W9-CHE-462

Montessori for the New Millennium

Dr. Maria Montessori, founder of the world-wide Montessori movement. Born August 31, 1870, Chiaravalle, Italy. Died May 6, 1952, Noorkwijk, Holland. The first woman in Italy to qualify as a doctor of medicine and Nobel Peace nominee.

Montessori for the New Millennium

*Practical guidance on the teaching
and education of children of all ages,
based on a rediscovery of the true principles
and vision of Maria Montessori*

Roland A. Lubienski Wentworth

LEA LAWRENCE ERLBAUM ASSOCIATES, PUBLISHERS
1999   Mahwah, New Jersey   London

© Original text copyright Felix Lubienski Wentworth

All texts quoted from published material of Dr. Maria Montessori, and photographs of her, © copyright, reproduced by kind permission of Association Montessori Internationale, Amsterdam, Netherlands.

Photographs of Montessori material kindly supplied by Nienhuis Montessori B. V., Zelhem, Netherlands

Copyright © 1999 by Lawrence Erlbaum Associates, Inc.
All rights reserved. No part of this book may be reproduced in any form, by photostat, microfilm, retrieval system, or any other means, without prior written permission of the publisher.

Lawrence Erlbaum Associates, Inc., Publishers
10 Industrial Avenue
Mahwah, NJ 07430

Cover design by Kathryn Houghtaling Lacey

Library of Congress Cataloging-in-Publication Data

Wentworth, Roland A. Lubienski.
Montessori for the new millennium / by Roland A. Lubienski Wentworth.

    p. cm.

Includes bibliographical references and indexes.
ISBN 0-8058-3136-3 (cloth : alk. paper)
1. Montessori method of education. I. Title.
LB1029.M75W46   1998
371.39'2—dc21   98-21723
                                                                                                              CIP

Books published by Lawrence Erlbaum Associates are printed on acid-free paper, and their bindings are chosen for strength and durability.

The final camera copy for this book was prepared by the author, and therefore the publisher takes no responsibility for consistency or correctness of typographical style.

Printed in the United States of America
10 9 8 7 6 5 4 3 2 1

This book is dedicated to the author's two grandchildren, Marc and Annabel, who represent the future generations for whom it was written.

The great help provided by Marc in the preparation of the text for publication is gratefully acknowledged.

Grateful thanks to Miss Alexandra Eversole, Headmistress for Gatehouse School, London, for permission to photograph in the school.

Errata

In the dedication: 'of', not 'for' Gatehouse
Page 47, para.2, line1:   delete 'be'
Page 97, para.2, line 11:   insert 'to' before 'meet'
Caption facing page 110:   add an 'e' to 'International'
Page 111, para.2, line 13: 'giving them what they need'
Page 116 page heading: delete 'Index', reposition '116'
Page 121, para.1, line 1:   'songs'

MONTESSORI FOR THE NEW MILLENNIUM

CONTENTS

Montessori's concept of the purpose of education. Scientific basis of educational technique. The heritage of Itard and Seguin expanded to embrace the whole field of education. Two fundamental concepts: deviations and normalization. Montessori's call to other educationalists to continue the educational research she started. The role of environment and its meaning.

The educational environment should provide conditions favorable to children's spontaneous activity. Characteristics of Montessori-oriented materials. Suggestions for teaching particular subjects. Importance of physical movement in the learning process.

Observation of free, unrestrained children led Montessori to discover their instinctive urge to become independent of the adult's help. The action of adult educators cannot reach the center of the children's learning functions, only the periphery, by providing suitable conditions for learning. The most important task of the teacher is to get the children interested. Movement should accompany and stimulate the work of the brain. Three main phases of children's development. The education of "Earth-children." Details of the educational program should be worked out within the framework of Montessori guidelines, but must be supplemented by experience. Planning and structure must be in conjunction with creativity and freedom of expression. The Montessori system is not a catalogue of established materials and teaching procedures, but a collection of correlated ideas, constantly open to checking and improvement. Common misconceptions about the Montessori system. Importance of keeping in touch with other educational systems and trends, and accepting sensible ideas from outside.

Montessori's answer to the discipline problem: give the child interesting, stimulating work. Mischievous, disruptive behavior cannot be tolerated. Creativity as a way of counteracting destruction. Dreikurs' three sources of children's' misbehavior and corresponding remedies. "Logical" consequences of disruption. The problem of hyperactive children. Troubles with noise. Collective misbehavior in groups of non-normalized children. Where compromises have to be made with children, parents, and the head of the school. Ways of silencing a noisy group. How to help children concentrate. Physical exercise on a rainy day. Moral influence through group meeting.

Spiritual preparation of the teacher. The teacher's "10 commandments." The algebra of the teacher's duties by Hélène Lubienska de Lenval. The teacher is like a salesman of educational ware. Dos and Don'ts. Marks and awards make children learn for the wrong reason and evaluate achievement, not effort. The educational value of children's meetings. The meeting's decisions should respect the interests of minority groups. Children's spontaneous organization to be encouraged. Suggestions for a timetable in a small school. Other suggestions. The teacher's role in forming the children's character.

The teacher and the aide. People who supervise and train the teachers. The role of parents in the school. Failings of some parent cooperative schools. Need for collaboration by all people concerned with children's education.

Montessori and the open classroom. Education of adolescents: the Erdkinder. Montessori-like education at Forest School, England.

Fundamental ideas of the Montessori system: positive attitude, and spiritual freedom. Montessori's vision of humanity transformed by the love of work.

Dr. Roland A. Lubienski Wentworth, PhD. Born July 22, 1900, Krakow, Poland. Died May 30, 1997, London, England. Disciple and personal friend of Maria Montessori. Inventor of the Lubienski "Maths Alive!" system for teaching mathematics the Montessori way.

Biographical Note on Roland Lubienski Wentworth

by Felix Lubienski Wentworth

Roland, my father, was born on July 22nd, 1900 in Krakow, in that part of Poland then ruled by the Austrian Empire, into an aristocratic Polish family traceable back to the 15th century. He was the great-great-grandson of the first Count Lubienski, a minister in the Grand Duchy of Warsaw, but the family was already illustrious as a result of having produced, over the centuries, no less than three archbishop-primates of Poland, and several bishops. He was the fourth of five children, four boys and a girl, and was baptized Zbigniew Antony Lubienski. Many years later, in 1947, having settled in England in 1933, and having just acquired British nationality, he adopted the additional surname of Wentworth, which had been the baptismal name of his great-uncle, Thomas Wentworth Lubienski. At the same time he officially changed his forename Zbigniew, which the English had always found unpronounceable, to Roland, by which name he had asked to be known ever since his first arrival in England. He never explained why he had chosen that name, but the closeness between the names Roland and Poland cannot have been altogether fortuitous.

His powerful intellect became apparent early on; and already in his teens he applied it to the study of philosophy, having declared his intention of entering holy orders. Whilst still not ordained he was sent to the Gregorian College in Rome to pursue his theological studies. But while there he gradually came to recognize that the strongly logical basis of his philosophical studies had displaced his religious faith, and so he felt he had no alternative but to abandon his intention of becoming a priest — the most difficult decision he ever had to make, he said. After a year spent in doing his military service in the cavalry, he enrolled in the philosophy department of Krakow's famed Jagiellon University, to study for a Ph.D. When he came to submit his thesis, which was on the English philosopher Thomas Hobbes, it was so long and detailed that before it could be accepted he had to cut it down to a quarter of its size. The thesis was subsequently published in full as a book, translated into German.

After graduating he became a lecturer in the same university department of philosophy; and subsequently, at the age of 28, he met and married another intellectual, who happened also to be a distant cousin, Countess Helen Czosnowska. It was she who, shortly afterwards, came under the spell of the great educationist, Maria Montessori, and together both of them then ardently followed her course of study. Always an idealist, my father saw in Montessori's revolutionary approach to education a new direction to follow in seeking to make the world a better place. They both became not only devoted disciples but close personal friends of hers as well. When I, their son Felix, was born, Maria Montessori consented to be my godmother, and from the outset my parents set about trying to raise me according to Montessori principles.

As their interest in the Montessori method deepened, each of them began to apply their own creative talent to it. Roland, who had always enjoyed math, recognized that many children acquire a life-long incomprehension and dislike of math, and he was convinced that this mental block could be avoided by using suitable manipulative materials of the kind Montessori had pioneered. He recognized that Montessori's basic bead material had limitations, and began to develop the use of 1-cm cubes instead, to create a whole new way of carrying the teaching of mathematics much further forward. To his great pleasure, it was a development that Montessori herself generously welcomed and encouraged. Much later he remembered a chance meeting that he had had as a boy on a train, with a psychic who foretold that one day he would create a great invention.

Despite this shared passionate interest, in personal terms he and my mother soon drifted apart. In 1933 on Montessori's recommendation Roland went to England to teach in a private progressive school, while my mother remained in France. Within a few years that physical separation was sealed by the Second World War. After the end of the war, their marriage was dissolved and later annulled. She too continued her dedication to Montessorian education, and published many books — including one entitled "La Méthode Montessori" on this theme, under the name Hélène Lubienska de Lenval (the "de Lenval" borrowed from her maternal grandfather), with an increasing interest in its application to the religious education of children. In 1955 Roland married again, this time to an Englishwoman, Phyllis Mason.

Throughout this period before, during and after the war, he taught in a wide variety of schools, always gaining further insights for his math teaching method, and for a time he worked as a lecturer, first in the Department of Education at Cambridge University and later at Bristol University. Of all those schools the one that came nearest to his ideal was one called Forest School, which had been founded in the New Forest, moved to Norfolk, and then sadly had to be closed down because of the war. Several of his own pupils at Forest School remained lifelong friends after they grew up. But always he remained true to his inspiration, the ideal of a Montessorian education for all, not just at nursery school age but throughout the formative years. For a time he served as a vice-chairman of the English Montessori Society. In his seventies, still amazingly active and full of hope, he went to America and in partnership with a businessman opened, in a suburb of New York, his own Wentworth School, at last fulfilling a long-held dream of putting these principles fully into practice. Alas his partner eventually let him down and the school had to close.

His life's work, namely the Lubienski math teaching method and material which Montessori herself had blessed, and which he greatly developed, patented, tested and proved in practice over many years, still awaits a wider audience. At the age of 90, still convinced that his method was something that the present technological age now needed more than ever, he set about updating it, giving it the new title "Math Alive!". I hope, in due course, to be able to bring this work to fruition.

Apart from his love of math, and an unusual clarity of thought, the unique contribution that Roland brought to his work with children was a childlike quality of his own that made him understand them exactly, and in turn made them look on him as their friend and equal, regardless of the difference in their ages. But he had friends of all ages, including many made in his later years, for he was the sort of unpretentious, unpompous person to whom people warm naturally. To all of them, great and small, he was simply "Roland". Always an active man, at the age of 94, while recovering in hospital from a leg embolism, he began, as a way of filling the time, to compose his memoirs, continuing to write these over the next two years, having mastered the use of a computer for this purpose, no mean feat for someone of that age. Under the title "Now That I'm Ninety-Four", these memoirs will be printed privately.

After all those years of doubt and agnosticism, his greatest consolation, in the last seven years of his life, was his return to the Catholic church, to which he had very nearly dedicated his life as a young man. Only in his last year, as a result of a series of small strokes, did Roland's intellectual powers gradually decline. These did not paralyze him but progressively incapacitated him. But even through the fog of those last days and weeks he remained gentle and appreciative, and on May 30th 1997, two months short of his 97th birthday, he died, peacefully and free from any pain. The last words he had written, in the epilogue to his memoirs, run as follows: "Unfortunately now my memory and concentration are beginning to fail me, and my legs seem increasingly reluctant to serve me. Ninety-six years is not, I think, a bad age to have reached. I have tried to use my time here to some purpose. And I hope that soon, with God's blessing, I may rest in peace."

His manuscript of the present book, as yet unpublished, was among his papers when he died. Together with the fruits of his seminal work in making math truly accessible to all children (and indeed to adults suffering from that all-too familiar "math block"), it shows that he did indeed use his time on earth "to some purpose".

Introduction

In the 1940s, there appeared a book called <u>Mathematics for the Million</u> by Lancelot Hogben. It was designed to place the abstruse realm of mathematics within everyone's reach. In looking for a title for this book, I thought at first of taking a leaf out of Hogben's and calling it <u>Montessori for the Million</u>, for my purpose is to show that the teachings of the great Maria Montessori are directly relevant to the education of everyone, at every level. But then, bearing in mind that we are rapidly approaching the millennium, which symbolizes the heralding of a new age, I decided to transmute it to <u>Montessori for the New Millennium</u>.

What is astonishing to me is that, although by now, in the late 1990s, the name of Montessori is almost universally known, and there are countless nursery schools throughout the world using the Montessori method, the real core of Montessori's thinking has continued to remain largely misunderstood. Most people regard the method as a system for the education only of children of *kindergarten* age. And most of those having some direct experience of it, whether as parent or teacher, would almost certainly regard this method as involving certain set procedures and a large amount of specialist material with elaborate instructions for its use. But in reality the essence of Montessori's philosophy of education was far broader than that, and contained a powerful message for all educationalists. In Montessori's mind it was a message that was relevant to the future of mankind as a whole.

I was fortunate enough to know Maria Montessori very well in the late 1920s and early 1930s, first as a disciple and later as a personal friend, and so had a unique opportunity of studying her system at its very source. Like many others I and my first wife, Hélène Lubienska de Lenval, were caught up in a wave of enthusiasm for the profound wisdom of her message. Under the influence of that message, I subsequently dedicated most of my life to working as a teacher, both in Montessori and traditional schools, and as a university lecturer. During this time I also wrote, lectured, and had many discussions with Montessori practitioners. At the same time, I gradually developed a whole new approach to the way mathematics is taught, based on Montessori's own embryonic thinking and from the outset with her personal approval and encouragement. I believe therefore that I am particularly well placed to bring together all the strands that made up her teaching and explain how they form a single, coherent view of education that is applicable to children of *all* ages and all cultures.

If I had to sum up the whole Montessori ideology in a single sentence, it would be that it is a guide to achieving a positive attitude of mind in all the circumstances of life. This principle pervades the whole Montessori system, which its founder saw clearly as something that applied not merely to nursery schools, but to the whole of education, from birth to maturity.

Believing that a positive mindset means focusing all one's thoughts, feelings, and actions on the positive, happy, and creative quality of life, and concentrating on the development of everything that makes life more enjoyable and happy, may seem like the empty aspirations of a mere idealist. Montessori was certainly an idealist, but she was a thoroughly practical one. She was very much interested in practical results, and lived to see thousands of nursery schools translate her principles into an everyday reality. As a qualified doctor, she approached the subject of education from the point of view of a scientist and a researcher. She saw a need to find practical ways of eliminating the feelings of scorn, hatred, jealousy, inadequacy, and rejection that are so characteristic, not only in much of our orthodox education but also, in consequence of that education, in our relations with each other in general in the adult world. She realized that it meant encouraging children instead of condemning them, stimulating their good impulses instead of repressing the bad ones, seeing the spark of good intentions and endeavors under a mountain of wrongdoing, and believing in the ultimate triumph of good, creative aspirations over lawlessness, vandalism, and destruction. She believed, in short, that a good mental disposition is an indispensable requirement for a happy, healthy, and efficient life.

Her idea was that by transforming the process of children's education she could help to transform the attitudes of the adults whom they would later become, and so those of society and the world at large. It was a breathtakingly bold yet practical, all-encompassing, positive vision of the potential of mankind on earth within a foreseeable future.

Today many fields of human endeavor have come to reflect the realization that people will be more ready to give their best and to perform better in their work if they are encouraged, listened to, and given a sense of "ownership" and responsibility than if they are simply told what to do. Industry has, under the leadership of such pioneers as Deming, taken this message to heart and as a result has witnessed a transformation in both industrial relations and efficiency. Only children's education still lags behind in this matter, the general policy of too many schools being immersed in the old practices of restraint, imposition, recrimination, and punishment — practices that are in reality counterproductive because they are completely opposed to the way in which young minds should be treated if their real potential is to be tapped.

The result is rebellion and hatred, instead of the positive, happy collaboration needed so badly by the world today. In the present conditions, a new teacher's task is regrettably, first and foremost, to learn how to control and constrain young "rebels" and force them to work, rather than learning how to develop the children's inborn — although sometimes hidden — desire for creativity and positive action, for becoming capable and skillful human beings and for building a better world.

Montessori started to reform the traditional practices, showing teachers how to reverse the usual negative attitudes and pessimistic outlooks on life, and encouraging them to have faith and trust in the younger generation. She pointed out, in particular, the need to use scientific methods for developing self-disciplined, happy, creative and positively directed minds.

Anyone studying Montessori's vast literary output must be struck by the fact that although her ideas only gradually developed throughout her long life, they always pursued strictly the same logical path. In all her numerous writings she never once contradicted herself, but only kept adding further remarks and observations that threw new light on her previously expressed opinions. She began by proving the effectiveness of such an approach at the pre-elementary level, which is the work for which she is most widely known. What is less well known is that she also strongly encouraged other educational leaders to extend this method to the higher levels of education. It is my purpose in this book to elucidate this

8

vital aspect of her life's work and to show how it applies to real-life teaching situations.

The suggestions made in the following pages apply chiefly to schools for children between the ages of 6 and 12, but when allowance is made for differences of age, ability, subjects of study, and other circumstances, the main guidelines apply even to those in older age groups. In following these guidelines drawn from a lifetime's experience of dealing with children, I show how the Montessori principles of positive education continue to be valid in the years following preschool. Contrary to many teachers' views, this is perfectly possible even though at that age, children's freedom is bound to be somewhat curtailed because they are expected to achieve certain standards required by society, with the laudable object of making the best use of their abilities and time during the years spent at school. In doing this, I hope I may be helpful not only to teachers but also to parents who, of course, want only the best for their children.

Finally, a brief semantic note about genders. Throughout this volume, in discussing any child, I tend to use the word "it", which satisfactorily signifies either a boy or a girl. In the quotations from Montessori, she generally referred to the child as "he", because in Italian there is no equivalent to "it." The meaning, however, is always "he or she." And when I talk about the role of the teacher, I generally use the word "he" because so much is drawn from my own experience, but again, the intention is always, of course, to mean "he or she".

1

The Principles of the Montessori System

One of the main ideas underlying the Montessori system was that education should fully develop children's positive potentials, so they can become happy and useful members of society. Like some of her eminent predecessors (e.g. Hume and Rousseau), Montessori believed the best way to achieve this was to see that education suits the child's nature and inclinations. To fulfill this purpose, she said, it is necessary to base the method on scientific principles drawn from firsthand investigation in schools.

Like all general statements and definitions, this brief summary of Montessori's intentions falls short of much that cannot be briefly explained, although the gist of them is therein[1]. Brought up in the early years of the growth of modern democracy, and imbued with the enthusiastic optimism that her early experiments with children seemed to justify, she firmly believed the result would support the liberalizing tendencies of the early 20th century; which is also perhaps why her system finds growing support in the late 1990s, in the postcolonial era with its strong emphasis on individual rights.

In Montessori's conception, the purpose of education is to help develop a free child, one who knows what it wants to be and do. She thought a free child would not later be inclined to accept dictatorial rule, nor to give in to the demands of an oppressive regime. She wrote:

> The child is the first part of the adult's life; indeed it is the builder of the adult. The good or the bad in the grown man is closely connected with the life of the child from which he came. The child is the whole of future humanity ... The social question of the child leads naturally to a desire to try to find out the laws of

man's formation, so helping us to create a new conscience and giving a new direction to our social life[2]

Montessori believed that nature has given children the right positive inclinations for becoming a happy member of a peaceful society, and that given favorable conditions, the child's positive qualities will develop and the ills of adult society will be cured. But one must distinguish between science and moral or social philosophy. As an educational scientist, Montessori could not take it on herself to decide what should be the political aims of educational development of a country. She could only indicate the most effective and psychologically sound method for bringing up well-integrated and happy human beings, able to form an integrated society. It would be for its members themselves to choose the type of social organization of which they would wish to be part. But would a generation of people brought up in freedom choose a regime that oppressed it? Montessori did not think so, hence her optimism for the future of a society educated in her schools[3].

This whole issue of free education had arisen long before Montessori. John Locke, in his book, Some Thoughts Concerning Education published in 1693, was the first to point out that teaching should vary according to the nature of the person taught, and that it should not have to be forced on people, because a lesson learned under pressure has only a superficial effect and is soon forgotten. Thus, we have known the truth of this statement for at least 300 years. But it was Montessori who discovered the way to make children learn while leaving them free[4]. She was one of the first to base her system on a scientific observation of children. She personally showed how to conduct an educational experiment scientifically, and encouraged future experiments of this kind to be carried out by others.

But neither her teaching aids, now summarily called the Montessori material, nor the technique of presenting them to the children, were her own inventions. Their originators were her French predecessors, Itard and Seguin, whose patient investigations were aimed at developing techniques for educating mentally handicapped children[5]. Montessori's main contribution was to point out the need to apply the same scientific process to normal boys and girls. The Itard-Seguin didactic methods used for

Dr. Jean-Marc-Gaspard Itard. Born 1775. Died 1838. French physician. One of Maria Montessori's two main precursors and sources of inspiration. From about 1800, became interested in teaching deaf and developmentally retarded children. Photo: Hulton Getty Picture Collection, London, England.

Dr. Edouard Séguin. Born January 20, 1812, Clamecy, France. Died October 28, 1880, New York City. French-born American psychiatrist. As a young man, he worked with Dr. Itard. In 1839 he opened a school for severely retarded children. To aid in teaching them he developed a variety of tactile material, which inspired Montessori. Photo: Economica, Paris, France.

mentally handicapped children led to a realization of two main facts: First, that children can learn to control their limbs and acquire elementary knowledge very much earlier than was previously believed; and second, that there are a number of distinct phases in children's development during each of which certain skills are more easily learned than either before or later, and each in turn making way for others.

Montessori supervised the first experiment on normal children in the famous Casa dei Bambini (Children's House) in Rome, and as a result of her inspiration and writings, similar preschool establishments, and further developments of the method, spread gradually worldwide. The experience gained in the preschools pointed the way to an extension of the method in two different directions: First, downward in age to babies from the very first days of their life; and second, upward in age to children of school age.

Montessori died in 1952, aged, respected, and admired by her many disciples. But the momentum of the movement for children's rights that she had started seems to have been lost through the double interruption of the two world wars, the banishment of her schools from Italy and Germany, and a general indifference on the part of official educational authorities everywhere. Since World War II, in particular, the new generation of educators and official lecturers has tended to regard Montessori as a figure belonging to the past, who of course had her place in the history of education, along with others such as Rousseau, Pestalozzi, and Froebel (whose teachings have already been assimilated into the modern theory of education), and are therefore no longer important — rather like those of the old philosophers whose ideas have by now been written down and classified, and have given way to new thinkers with their own original theories. Yet despite this indifference, Montessori schools and training colleges have somehow survived and continued their work in the private sector; and as if the death of the old pioneer acted to remind educational circles of their existence, a revival of the Montessori movement started to take place, chiefly in America, in the early 1950s, backed by modern writers in educational psychology. The experiments of Piaget, the new educational guru, confirmed the existence of phases in the development of the child's mind and comprehension. The stage was set for "the method" to come out of the closet of the private sector into the open field of public education.

In our modern world, beset by problems that recurrently assume international proportions, it has become common (and with good reason, too) to put the blame for most social evils on inadequate education. However, the educational theories of our age seem to swing between two extremes: excessive rigidity on the one hand and chaos on the other, neither of which is able to cope with the problems of present day society. The Montessori system lies roughly between the two extremes. Based not only on sound general theory but also tested in solid practical classroom experience, it offers freedom without anarchy, and discipline without rigidity.

One fact clearly stands out: Apart from some experiments made during her time spent in India, Montessori was never able to create a complete well-tested school program for children ages 6 to 9 or older. Hence, whatever materials and methods are used for children of mandatory school age, they should be subjected to the same degree of scientific investigation as were the Montessori preschools. And even the preschools themselves, if they are to reflect truly the spirit of Montessori education, should be undergoing continual revision and modification according to the changing times and different needs of new generations of children. This principle has to some extent been recognized by Montessori schools in the United States and in a number of other countries by the introduction of a more diversified environment and a number of new, Montessori-oriented materials. However, the original implements and methods introduced by Itard and Seguin, such as the sensorial apparatus, movable alphabet letters, and the beads for arithmetic, are still the predominant feature.

Because there is no established pattern to show how an elementary school is to be run on Montessori lines, and Montessori is no longer here to guide us, the only way to found a school that can justifiably be called Montessorian is to examine some of the characteristics inherent in the environment, materials and method used in the Montessori preschool, to see if they could conceivably be applied to the education of older children. Qualified educators need to investigate and test the value of various educational materials and methods and discuss it openly among themselves. But not all teachers are suited for such research. Therefore, the question of whether some material or teaching practice genuinely reflects the Montessori ideal, and whether it has a desirable effect on children, is something that needs to be explored by academic institutions with experts in educational research.

It is important to stress that in general educational terminology the term Montessori education does not signify any particular proprietary rights or franchise attached to some particular material or teaching device, but rather a type of education, a set of principles, and a philosophy associated with and reflected in the works of Maria Montessori. Conceiving it in this way, it is possible to imagine a teacher creating a Montessori school even in a jungle, far away from civilized life and without any resources for buying Montessori materials from a factory. She would use her ingenuity, and whatever raw materials were available in the vicinity, to produce "tools" appropriate to the children's needs in relation to the level of civilization in which they were going to live. In the same way, it is perfectly possible for a poor village school in a civilized country, unable to purchase any standard Montessori equipment, to apply the general principles of the method and provide such materials as can be bought cheaply or made by the teacher's own hands, thus creating a genuine Montessori environment.

The name Montessori is in a way like that of Froebel, whose kindergartens (children's gardens) became even more famous than Montessori's Children's Houses. Who would expect the Froebel Institute to keep uniquely to the materials and methods Froebel had introduced? The Froebel schools support everything that in their opinion is good for the child, thus entering into the spirit of their founder's prescriptions, and as a result achieving standards far above anything dreamed of by Froebel himself. But in following Montessori's footsteps, there is more than a general idea to interpret. There are definite principles and specific educational practices tested many times in schools in various countries and at different levels of civilization.

When a visitor, entering a classroom, finds the children walking on a painted line round the room, or sitting motionless, almost holding their breath during a lesson of silence, or deeply immersed in some calculation with the help of little seeds or stones, he will recognize that it is a Montessori classroom — even if none of the classical beads, bells, or colored tablets are in use. But even if none of these traditional practices are to be seen, there are some general directives, some specific rules based on an intimate knowledge of children's nature and proved in their efficacy, which make a Montessori classroom what it is: a children's community, with a teacher discreetly in the background, a place free from unnecessary restrictions, and yet disciplined, with children enjoying work without being compelled to do it — a true miracle as it was called when it was first seen in the San Lorenzo slum district of Rome.

Here I discuss what are these specific rules and principles, that give Montessori schools their particular character.

The highlights of the system were brilliantly summarized by Montessori in a series of six talks she gave at the Montessori International Conference in Amsterdam, Holland in 1933. I have in my possession the transcript of five of these lectures in French, together with a summary of the sixth made by my first wife Hélène Lubienska de Lenval. The following pages are based on those manuscripts.

First, Montessori said that nature has provided the child with an instinct that gives it a powerful urge to explore the surrounding world and become independent of grown-up help. It is that same instinct that drives birds to try their wings to fly, and compels all young animals to search for food, shelter, and the satisfaction of their various needs independently of their parents. Fully-grown animals do not oppose this tendency in their young, do not hinder their development by overprotection, but often help it. Thus, birds push their young out of the nest when the time is ripe, ducks lead their ducklings into the water, and so on. Human adults often fail to understand this tendency in their children, and either stop them from exploring their surroundings or hinder their movements by confining them to narrow playpens and cots and tight clothes, or by feeding them, dressing them, and doing most things for them instead of letting them learn how to do these tasks for themselves. As a result, those children do not develop normally but instead become frustrated, bored, discouraged, and angry, and may acquire the negative traits by which they are commonly known such as unreasonable behavior, changing moods, crying, impatience, mischievousness, disobedience, and laziness.

The way to prevent these DEVIATIONS, as Montessori called them, is to provide children with a suitable environment in which they are able to learn to be independent, without being hindered by grown-ups. A deviated child can become "cured" if it is put into a suitable environment while it is still at a receptive age (normally before it is 4 or 5 years old).

Second, if the environment is to have its effect, the parent or teacher must not be in a commanding position, like a dictator, compelling children to do certain jobs or assignments under threat of penalties. A Montessori educator should be like a waitress, who faces her customers, offers them the menu and serves them well-prepared dishes, or like a laboratory assistant who introduces the students to the right way of handling scientific apparatus, or a librarian who gives the readers the required guidance for finding the books they desire. Montessori called the resulting change produced in deviated children through this way of teaching, NORMALIZATION. It is a condition in which the child and educator work in unison, without opposition. The child works freely and happily with the materials supplied to it, at a pace suiting its own nature, without the motivation of rewards and punishments, or being spurred unduly by competition, or compelled by the requests of the teacher.

Montessori used the term Normalization because of her conviction that putting a child in a proper, natural environment, will enable it to revert to its "normal," sociable self, thus ending any further trouble for educators.

This conversion begins the moment the child becomes deeply immersed in an occupation, and as a result develops a power of concentration and acquires a love of learning and acquiring new skills. The child becomes independent, self-disciplined, responsible, happy, and sociable. Thus, a salient characteristic of the Montessori method is that character building goes hand in hand with intellectual development, so that one is an essential concomitant of the other.

As the child becomes addicted to work, its character changes for the better. Montessori believed the first step toward sensible education is to keep the child in its normal condition and, if the child is already deviated, to normalize it. All other guidelines, namely the creation of an appropriate environment, the provision of suitable materials, enabling the child to progress at its own pace, and so forth, are dictated by the fact that they lead to and maintain a normalized state of mind.

But the methods must be of a positive kind, by encouraging and gently stimulating, because negative methods cause opposite reactions and hinder the development of positive and creative energies. Helping children too much, or providing them with ready answers to problems, is also a negative factor because it prevents the child from using its own resources for knowledge acquisition, and deprives the child of the pleasure of discovery.

Montessori considered her own achievements as only the beginning of a scientific and exploratory process of educational investigation that should be continued by other educational workers:

> This book of methods, compiled by one person alone, must be followed by many others. It is my hope that, starting with the individual study of the child educated by our method, other educators will publish the results of their experiments. These will be the pedagogical books which await us in the future[6].

In time, therefore, the whole environment of the Montessori class may become just "Montessori-oriented," without any of the original materials remaining, yet nonetheless true to the main line laid down by its author. Moreover, once we agree that children should be brought up as free agents, devoted to working on their own accord, without compulsion, there is no reason to stop at the preschool, or even at the elementary school level. A logical follow-up to a Montessori preschool would be first an elementary, then a high school, and a university, all run the same, so that a normalized society would be the end result.

Obviously teaching at these different levels must vary according to the age and interests of the pupils. A complication arises because teaching must take into account the official school curriculum. Children in private Montessori schools cannot be allowed to study what they like to the extent of neglecting what other youngsters have to learn in the public sector. Therefore, ways must be found to attract these children to a whole range of subjects without making them feel compelled to learn them. Montessori solved the problem brilliantly at the preschool stage, teaching children to read and write and do simple number work before the age when those in other schools have even begun to learn the first letters. It can perhaps be argued that a phonetic language such as Italian may not present the same difficulties in spelling as does English. But an adaptation of the method to the English language has been worked out successfully by Montessori' s followers. Some arithmetic and whole sections of grammar can be taught by lively and <u>interesting manipulative exercises</u>. Likewise it has been suggested for teaching history (including prehistoric periods), geography, and science. Anna Maccheroni and other authors have worked out fascinating ways of teaching music to young children. Still, most of these rather sporadic contributions do not represent a systematic and comprehensive elementary approach. They are activities likely to add interest to the study of various subjects, but are not as comprehensive as the conventional lesson program. And the higher one reaches, looking for truly Montessorian ways of learning, the more haphazard are the exercises, the less visible the direct influence of Montessori, and the less difference there is between practices used in Montessori high schools and their conventional counterparts. The battle is far from being won, and a united effort on the part of both schools and teachers is needed if further, and constant, improvement is to be assured.

In order to leave the children free, and yet teach them whatever they may need for their future work in society, the Montessori method creates a structured environment, that leads children indirectly, instead of giving them direct lessons and instruction by the teacher. The environment gives the child the opportunity of learning in the way suited to its nature, without undue interference by the teacher, except when the learner calls for it himself.

The next chapter discusses in detail what the environment of an elementary Montessori class should be like. The general principles of the method and Maria Montessori's own hints and suggestions expressed in various writings and lectures should be kept in mind.

2

The New Environment

How do we discover the best kind of environment for an elementary school-age child? The <u>Dottoressa</u> (as the Italians used to call Montessori) offered the following account of the way she discovered the right environment for preschool children:

It was January 6th (1906), when the first school was opened for small, normal children of between three and six years of age. I cannot say on my methods, for these did not yet exist. Though the school contained some really wonderful toys, the children never chose them. This surprised me so much that I myself intervened, to show them how to use such toys, teaching them how to handle the doll's crockery, lighting the fire in the tiny doll's kitchen, setting a pretty doll beside it. The children showed interest for a time, but then went away, and they never made such toys the objects of their spontaneous choice. And so I understood that in a child's life play is perhaps something inferior, to which it has recourse for want of something better, but that there were loftier things which, in the child's mind, seemed to take precedence over useless amusements[7].

As a result of such reflections, Montessori said:

The environment we have prepared for the child is designed to stimulate spontaneous activity (while as a rule we wish to stimulate only activities we want children to learn); as a result we discovered some children's characteristics which we didn't expect to find in a child, such as concentration, self-discipline, and a love of work[8].

Illustrating the idea by a concrete example, she suggested:

Using faucets with care (Gatehouse School, London).

Keeping the classroom clean. Note the child-sized broom, chairs, and table (Gatehouse School) Photos: Scott Thompson, London.

If a child shows some interest in an object, let it handle it as long as possible, and it will busy itself with it for hours. Try the following method with the little jesters who, for example, leave the tap running although you have told them a thousand times they must not touch it. On the contrary, let them touch the tap, but show them exactly how to use it, then leave them alone and observe them discreetly. You will see that they will take great care in using it properly and that they will not touch it any more once they have satisfied their curiosity[9].

Although in the previous quotations Montessori obviously had a small child in mind, experience shows that what she said applies to children of any age — maybe even to adults. In a grade school, of course, we cannot have unlimited choice because we have to follow the school's curriculum. Thus, every teacher must make his own choice in deciding which books or other materials to provide so the children can acquire some particular skills or knowledge in various individual subjects. Some children may respond to certain materials, other children to others. But we must have sufficient materials that appeal to all children in order to give them an incentive for creative work. From my personal experience I have compiled some lists of items for a Montessori elementary class. These are found in the appendix. The list begins with the most important items. These are followed up with more detailed specifications.

General Observations

Even though it seems obvious, it cannot be emphasized too strongly that the classroom, indeed the whole school building and its surroundings, should be attractive, homey, reasonably clean, easy to keep tidy (assuming that the children are expected to help in tidying it at least once a day after school), warm in cold weather, cool on hot days, consisting of nice room proportions (the ceiling should be fairly high to allow plenty of air, but windows low and plentiful), with desks and chairs varying according to the children's sizes, and plenty of nice colors everywhere. It is surprising how often the appearance of the classroom is neglected, although there can be no doubt that it has a profound effect on the general feeling and behavior of children.

It is not advisable to have the same pictures on the walls throughout the entire year. After a while, neither the teacher nor the children notice them any more (unless they are things referred to in the school program, such as diagrams of the body or maps). Replacing the pictures from time to time will result in the pictures being noticed.

Ample storage space should be provided, either in the classroom or nearby. Frequently used materials should be kept within easy reach of the children, whereas others are better kept in dustproof cupboards, with labels clearly indicating where each item should be located.

Children of postkindergarten level are not likely to spend much time clearing away materials consisting of many different items, therefore, it saves trouble both for them and for the teacher to have the work simplified as much as possible. Two boxes could be substituted in cases where the manufacturer provided only one, or a much larger box can be utilized to contain the items more loosely. Most boxes with materials purchased in shops are too flimsy and fall apart in a matter of weeks. These boxes should be replaced with something stronger (but not less attractive) before any items are lost.

The arrangement of desks, pictures, and so on can be very helpful, and children should be consulted. They will be more likely to keep a certain order if they have contributed to the decision of how to arrange the classroom.

Regardless of which materials are on view in the classroom, it is important to remember the Montessori principle of a controlled (i.e. limited) environment. Children surrounded by too many materials find it difficult to make a choice. Teachers who know their preferences can keep a limited number of appropriate alternatives in front of them and be ready to change them when a child's interest begins to fade. But as children tend to have a gregarious instinct and often all wish to do the same thing, especially if it is something new, a sufficient number of similar items should be provided, so several pupils can be occupied with the same work. For instance, there may be enthusiasm for weaving, or working with clay, tracing maps, doing jigsaw puzzles and so on. If teachers stick too rigidly to the principle adopted in the preschool Montessori class that there should be only one set of each item per class and make children wait for their turn, the desire to use the material may fade, and the chance of using the collective enthusiasm for the activity will be lost.

One more suggestion: Many schools require children to leave all outdoor footwear in the hall and to wear light shoes or sneakers or stay in socks inside the classroom. This is a good habit, both for hygienic reasons and because it saves much of the clean-up after school.

To avoid cluttering this chapter with too much mundane detail, the appendix lists my suggestions for both outdoor and indoor equipment, that should be obtained by a Montessori school.

It is not enough to have a fine environment and a good collection of teaching materials. The teacher must be able to apply them. In order to do this the teacher must develop various techniques and planning details and learn to solve different problems, according to the circumstances in which the teaching takes place. In the following pages, I outline a few suggestions regarding the teaching of various subjects at elementary level. These may be useful to teachers.

Writing and Reading

It would be ideal if all newcomers to the Montessori primary school had previously been trained in a good Montessori preschool, consequently learning to read and write reasonably fluently. Unfortunately, in practice this is often not the case; there often are several children who barely know a few letters of the alphabet, and even these were taught nonphonetically (ay, bee, cee, etc.) The classroom may not even have the Montessori equipment concerned, or if so primary school age children may not respond to the Montessori approach devised for 3- to 4-year-olds. Also, it may be impossible to devote the necessary time to teach children writing and reading without neglecting the rest of the class who may be more advanced. In that case, the teacher has to resort to other methods devised for older children. Preferably, the methods do not require too much of the teacher's attention. Some publishers offer excellent sets of easy readers, of gradually increasing difficulty, accompanied by reinforcement and word-recognition pads, that lead the children slowly but surely through all the hurdles of reading and spelling. Care must be taken, however, to ensure the size of letters for beginners is fairly large, especially for dyslexics. As for writing, children like tracing letters and numbers, and can easily be persuaded to trace pages from their reading books. But it is very important that they begin tracing each letter or figure in the right sequence, because wrong habits are difficult to eradicate. Some teachers may prefer using different methods — anything is good that works!

After 6 months (or maybe sooner) of such training, children should be ready for exercises in spelling. In this matter, the series of "Skills in Spelling" published by McCormick-Mathers is one of the best. It also teaches children to write in cursive script. The "organic spelling" method described by Ashton-Warner in "Teacher" is worth noting, too — perhaps in addition to other systems. She asked the children to give her a number of words — any that came into their heads, without thinking. She wrote these words on little cards, and gave them to the children to read. All cards were then thrown together into a basket, and the children were asked to find "their" word cards again. The next day the exercise was repeated — maybe with the addition of further words. Because these words have real meaning for each child, coming from its subconscious, it remembers their spelling without difficulty[10].

Controversy exists as to whether children should be allowed to write their own stories before they can spell the words correctly. In my opinion, creativeness is more important than correct spelling, and children should be encouraged to write their ideas in any form — as long as they can be read afterward. The teacher should not attempt to correct spelling in such organic stories unless the child expressly asks for it — otherwise the child may feel the teacher is interfering with its most intimate experiences and thoughts. The teacher can, however, make note of some of the child's typical spelling errors and later provide some corrective exercises.

Math

There are many divergent opinions in this field. Should children proceed from concrete to abstract? Should they first be allowed to use blocks before using graphic signs? Should they be told the reasons for each operation or merely taught the way to proceed, like the rules of a game?

Should teachers start with the set theory and simple nondecimal bases before teaching the whole decimal system? How much "new math" should children learn in comparison with traditional mathematics?

Personally, I prefer to follow the middle course: The new math can be taught and blocks can be used as long as the children like them, but this method should not be overdone either. Children should not be given complicated exercises without any relevance to real life while they are still unable to understand addition and subtraction. Teachers should not insist on using concrete materials if the children would rather do their sums without them. Some children grasp abstract numbers easily, thus excessively working with concrete materials would unnecessarily retard their progress.

On the other hand, some manipulative experience in the beginning does help even the naturally gifted mathematicians understand math, and assists them in their later progress. I once had the rare privilege, at the Gatehouse Montessori School in London, of giving elementary mathematics lessons to a 6-year old boy who quickly manifested a phenomenal mathematical ability that enabled him to advance by leaps and bounds and solve even the trickiest problems without difficulty. At the age of 14, this boy participated in the International Mathematics Olympiad in Bulgaria, where the average age of the other participants was 19. Although he was the youngest participant, he won first prize, getting full marks in the competition. During his 8 years of Montessori training, he had been sitting in the same class with a mixed group of children of different abilities and ages — some of them with Down syndrome — but was allowed to pursue math lessons at his own pace. In the early stages he did, like the others, show visible interest in the structural materials, although he soon outpaced the other children and moved easily into pure abstractions. It is difficult to judge the extent to which the early concrete manipulations aided the phenomenal progress of his later years, but it is certain that children feel a kind of mental torture when trying to deal with figures without any concrete equivalent. Their replacement by tangible materials, even temporarily, becomes a real necessity.

In a subject such as mathematics, one can easily become doctrinaire by trying to enforce a program that is neither enticing nor necessary for the child's future. Being able to add correctly long columns of numbers was once considered important. This requirement became obsolete with the invention of pocket calculators. In the late 1990s, there are computers that can rapidly perform even the most difficult mathematical operations. That does not mean that the need to teach mathematics no longer exists. There remains the need to know which operation to use. The old insistence, however, to "know your tables" is no longer as relevant. Mathematics is important, more than ever in our era, but it is senseless to try to outdo its mechanical tools, which are meant to save time and labor. If a child asks me the answer to 8 x 7, my answer is: "Find out for yourself, using concrete materials — or else look it up." Generally speaking, I prefer to give the children easy sums — with answers not exceeding 100 — and ask them to solve a lot of practical problems from real life, but still using small numbers that can be easily checked in one's head. I also have them do a lot of measuring, geometrical drawings, manipulating geometrically shaped objects, and passing from concrete to abstract to show that operations with figures written on paper are only symbolic representations of corresponding manipulative procedures. Mathematics then appears as something sensible, related to life, and not an abstract game with increasingly complicated rules.

There may be limits to such concrete representation of abstract calculations. But a substantial proportion of students, to say the least, seem to favor this kind of approach and, once the foundations of mathematics are explained in this way, find it easier to proceed further without "concretization". Montessori demonstrated that such manipulative preparation allows the teaching of mathematics at an earlier age — without the risk of holding back potential geniuses such as the talented Gatehouse School pupil I have mentioned.

Geography

Geography can be called the study of "man and his environment" or inversely "the Earth and what man has made of it." It is a vast subject, that can be tackled from many angles. Children can be asked to trace and enlarge maps; draw sketches of the interior of the school, apartment or district of the town; draw graphs; make 3-dimensional models of geographical features in clay and plaster; learn how the type of landscape, climate, vegetation, and so on influences the ways of living and earning a living; make little dolls and dress them with paper clothes according to the customs in various parts of the world, and many other similar exercises.

There are some excellent social studies books that enable children to work individually and enjoy doing so. The teacher's inventiveness and imagination can add further ideas and give the children both erudition and enjoyment.

It may seem logical to start by studying the immediate environment, the layout of the school, the hometown and country before learning about the more distant territories and overseas continents, but sometimes greater interest is aroused through a study of exotic lands and peoples first. The clue for an interesting lesson may also be given by a casual incident, a political event, or catastrophe, providing an opening for follow-up talks, discussions, and resulting essays or some practical work. This may even lead the way for further investigation in various directions. However, this kind of sporadic teaching does impose great demands on the teacher and becomes difficult, if not impossible, if each child is allowed to work individually at its own pace. It lends itself, therefore, more to occasional talks and collective projects than to a regular way of working throughout the school year. Hence as a normal course of action, it seems safer to let children follow the exercises of a good set of workbooks, with occasional digressions when the opportunity arises.

The study of geography seems incomplete without astronomy, especially if children can be taken out to study the stars and various constellations, learn to find directions, or tell the time at night by watching the position of the stars. At a time when the discoveries made by astronauts and unmanned satellites are so frequently in the news, children should not be left unaware of these events.

History

Montessori was particularly fond of history, and gave many suggestions about the way that it should be approached. She thought children should study the history of the formation of the earth and the planets, the evolution of life, the history of inventions, explorations, and discoveries, especially while they are at an age when the urge for adventure is very strong. Stories about the past can be brought to life by drawings, making old-fashioned costumes, play-acting, and so on. Some schools have the children make a long strip presenting historical events at proportionate distances from each other. The strip is rolled like a scroll at each end around a stick. The difficulty arises when one moves far back in time, describing events in early history or prehistory, where we have little information and the scroll would have to be impossibly long to be kept in the right proportion of time.

Nature Study

In the case of nature study, the opportunity for study by action is better than in any other subject. Children can grow plants from seeds in glass containers, observe the growing of stems, leaves, and roots; and see how the flower changes into fruit and seeds, thus completing the cycle. The study of animals can begin by observation and maintenance of various pets kept in the classroom. They can learn anatomy by examining their own bodies, watching the muscles become tense and relaxed, their chests expand by breathing, feeling the beating of their hearts, and so on. Excursions into the country and visits to botanical and zoological gardens and museums can help widen the knowledge acquired at school.

Science

Both physics and chemistry can be taught by letting children carry out carefully graded experiments, beginning with very young children. An important condition for individual study is the creation of a good but simple laboratory provided with some essential substances and materials (such as water, salt, sugar, a lever, a pulley, a magnet, a few lenses, batteries, wire, bulbs, etc.), so that all the items needed for an experiment can be preassembled, and applied by the child without help from the teacher. There are several publications that offer necessary guidance and are inexpensive. The chief difficulties, however, lie in wording the instructions so that they can be understood by even small children without constant help, or the maintenance of a supply of materials, by the teacher. Children need to have a certain maturity and be able to work independently before they can work in a laboratory without too many problems.

Language

Montessori showed how even the tedious study of grammar can be turned into fun by combining the activity of the mind with manual procedures such as placing symbols cut out of colored paper under corresponding parts of speech. If such ingenious conceptions are to go beyond casual, sporadic exercises, however, they must be complemented by systematic study, which means using some kind of textbook or workbook.

The trend in the 1990s is to require children at an early age to learn, in addition to their mother tongue, one or more foreign languages. There are many valid reasons for this practice. A child, who has after all learned to speak its own native language fluently in just a few years by ear alone, can master other languages with equal ease. Even if such study does not go very deep, and is soon forgotten without constant practice, it is possible that a good intonation and accent get buried somewhere in the subconscious, and will return when serious learning begins at some point later. The main difficulty lies in finding teachers who possess a sufficient fluency and correct accent in the spoken language that they can be relied on not to make any mistakes. I have met teachers who incorrectly taught children to pronounce the German word das Boot (the boat) like the English word "boot," or call "the mouse" in French le souris, forgetting that its gender is feminine (la souris), no matter whether it is a male or a female mouse. Teaching a language with markedly wrong pronunciation or mistakes defeats its own purpose. An extensive use of tapes or cassettes made by native speakers is too formal for children of elementary school age. Such methods certainly have a place, but they cannot entirely compensate for the lack of a good teacher. In such cases, the best way is to arrange for the child to stay abroad for a time, or give it an opportunity to play with children of the other nationality. This allows the child to learn the foreign tongue in the same way as it learned its own.

Thus far, the discussion has focused only on "academic" subjects contained in the curriculum of most public schools. Naturally we would want to see that the children in our own Montessori-type school attain the same standards of achievement as are required in public schools, if only to stop gifted children from having to leave the Montessori school at 12 to continue their studies elsewhere. The same applies to practical skills such as art in its various ramifications, dancing and music (instrumental and vocal), drama, and so on. Montessori expressed her admiration for the practice of sports and preferred them to pure physical training drills, which offer little incentive and practically no activity for the brain (see her article in "Montessori Notes," London, issue of October 1935). However, she did not approve of overstraining children's capacity through exaggerated competition and attaching too much importance to beating another team, or to being the best in the class or school.

There are many other subjects and skills that children may find both interesting and useful later in life. In an age of growing demand for gender equality, both boys and girls should have the opportunity to learn the rules of behavior at home, in school (as in a future office), and in the street (e.g. how to cross the road), prevention of accidents, fire precaution rules, how to use a first-aid box, common measures for keeping healthy and strong, typing, duplicating, printing, general house maintenance, cooking, sewing, room decorating, and carpentry, together with the proper use of tools, how to mend fuses and do simple repairs around the house, understanding the mechanics of a car, radio, TV, and so on.

Montessori rightly stressed the importance of teaching about money and its uses. She said children should learn to appreciate the value of money by getting an opportunity to earn it. A significant article on this subject appeared in "Montessori Notes" of May/June 1934. But in the late 1990s, when international travel has become common, necessitating a knowledge of currency exchange, changes of time and of units of measure, and when financial crises can diminish the value of money, not to speak of periods of unemployment and so on, children should also be taught about investments, interest rates, inflation, insurance, and different ways of earning money, for example. One suggestion is to set up a school bank, connected perhaps with one of the local banks that would agree to pay interest calculated on a daily basis. Children would be able to put in their savings and see how much they can earn by not spending their money all at once.

One important thing should be remembered in all teaching. As is shown in the next chapter, Montessori stressed that physical movement stimulates the brain, makes learning easier, more attractive, and better remembered. It is therefore characteristic of all teaching in Montessori schools that as far as possible some physical movement accompanies the learning process. It is of course particularly useful for mentally handicapped or dyslexic children, but all can benefit from this practice.

In view of the growing number of useful materials and ideas for making learning more effective and enjoyable, it would be useful to have more interchange of ideas not only between Montessori-type schools, but also with other progressive schools. An Educational Consumers Association could be formed to issue bulletins with descriptions and an unbiased evaluation of new creative teaching devices, together with an indication of places where the use of them can be observed in action and where relevant materials can be acquired.

In the foregoing pages I have listed only the physical part of the environment. However important it is, it would be ineffective without its counterpart in the social and spiritual atmosphere provided, through the way that education is organized and how it is influenced by the teacher, by the community of children in the class, and by the people in charge of them. I deal with these questions in the next chapters.

3

Creativity and Structure

The following examines some specific passages in Montessori's writings that refer to the methodology of teaching. How her ideas can be applied in both elementary and high schools is discussed.

To start with some recapitulation: The point of departure in Montessori's pedagogy is the observation of children's spontaneous behavior when they are without constraint:

> If a new and scientific pedagogy is to arise from the study of the individual, such study must occupy itself with the observation of free children[11].

The first thing that comes to light from the observation of free children is (as stated before) that:

> A child has an irresistible natural tendency to grow. He cannot renounce it to adapt himself to social conventions. He defends himself against everything that prevents his energy from expanding, because he must at all costs grow — otherwise he would die. If he adapts himself partially . . . he will grow into an improperly developed and weakened individual[12].

The child has no time to lose:

> for his work consists in building up an adult individual, and he has to complete it in a definite period of time; he can neither speed up the process nor have it done by someone else[13].

The conclusion that follows is that:

> It is the child who builds up the man, the child alone. The adult cannot take his place in this work[14].

This is a concept of learning as an organic process which cannot be forced by interference from outside. This is further explained by an analogy with the center and the periphery of a figure:

> Since it is the mind that organizes itself through its continuous activity as center, while at the periphery are the senses and the movement . . . it is only the periphery of the whole activity that is accessible to us.

> Our task as educators places us at the periphery as directors. We shall not abandon the child to lonely researches in an overcomplicated world; no, we shall prepare and set ready for him — at the periphery — within his reach, a world restricted to his needs. We shall thus suit ourselves to his attitude, interpreting these needs by the way he manifests them — at the periphery . . .

> We leave the center free to develop in harmony with natural forces. We need neither to know about the center, nor to expect it to react for us. Our business is respect for the center[15].

But the child

> resists interference by the adult who thinks he can help him by his power. For this uncalled-for interference upsets its natural rhythm and prevents nature from accomplishing its task . . . For the child to grow and develop, the authority of the grown-up must decrease[16].

Montessori was very firm about this principle of noninterference. She said: "Every time the adult helps the child unnecessarily, he stops or thwarts its development[17]."

In an article entitled "Advice to Teachers" (called by Montessori directresses) published in <u>Montessori Notes</u> of March 1935, she gave a valuable indication of the role the educator must play in helping the child. Although she was referring to the Exercises in Practical Life, the principles she laid down apply to all learning activities. The teacher

> must let the children work at these exercises if they want to, even for the whole day if they wish it; only she should make the other work so interesting that they will not wish to devote themselves

exclusively to one thing. She should not, however, become alarmed even if the children give themselves up exclusively for several days to one kind of work: this is what we call an "explosion"; and this continuous application to one kind of work — provided it is done with intensity, that is to say, with sincerity — always produces the best results ... She should point out every detail of the action with absolute clearness, and then leave the child the means of perfecting himself, without correcting him, even if he does it badly. What is important is that the child should do the work himself without a word, or other assistance — not even a glance — from the directress.

She must give her lesson; plant the seed in the soil, and then slip away; observe and wait expectantly, but not interfere ... — If the material interests him, the child will repeat the exercise and this repetition of the exercise develops not only intelligence but also character; therefore the progress of the class, as well as its discipline, depends on the interest of the children in their work.

Further advice to the teachers was given in Montessori's introduction to "Psychogeometry":

The art of learning depends on one condition — and it is an essential one — the learner's desire to learn and his attention — in short, his interest. The indispensable condition for success is that his mind should be at work; all that bores and discourages interrupts this psychic activity and builds up a barrier that no mere logical perfection of the teaching art can ever surmount .... Nothing can be assimilated without effort, we grant; ... But effort is the bringing into action of the individual's entire energy, and this happens only where interest is felt. Man is no machine — he acts inspired by interest — generosity — enthusiasm; and he will then throw himself with all his life, strength and activity into this effort — even if it is irksome. An educator who succeeds in evoking interest — interest leading to choice of some action and the carrying out of it with the whole energy of the chooser, all his constructive enthusiasm — such an educator has awakened a man to life.

Undreamed-of forces reveal themselves very often in one whose interest has been evoked. The child spurred on by interest will display powers latent till then or never guessed at[18].

Throughout the process of education, one feature is of primary importance: The mental effort should be accompanied by a physical one because the latter is needed to stimulate the action of the brain. Hence it is unnatural to use one without the other. In an article on the organization of movement, Montessori wrote:

Lately movement has come into education as a necessity, but not as a factor with which to help the building of intelligence, only as a rest from mental fatigue, which was supposed to be so great that movement was rendered obligatory in the form of gymnastics.

The idea that muscular fatigue separated from mental fatigue can be a rest from the latter is wrong. Why should one fatigue be a rest from another? The fatigue arises from the fact that mental and motor activity which should form one unity are found separate. If the individual does not succeed in becoming unified in such a way that his mind works with movement (and the mind helping to direct the movement is at the same time helped by the movement), every effort is felt as fatigue. This is the reason why a movement which is imposed and ordered, such as gymnastics, cannot be restful.

As a further step came sport, which concentrates movements in a precise direction, that is, each sport aims to reach a certain purpose, so that the 'interior will' and the 'motor will' fuse together. Intelligence and sentiment act together, and this kind of synthesis makes sport superior to gymnastics . . .

Movement must be extended through all the phases of life and not occur only at special moments, and above all it is important that movement is considered as a necessity, as a necessary co-operation to the mental and moral development, especially in childhood, when the development of personality takes place.

Movement is important because it allows the individual to attain the functional unity between psychic and external action, that is, the unity of personality.

Lastly, movement must not only be considered useful to physical life but indispensable to the psychic life. So that intelligence may develop normally, so that character and moral sense may also develop, it is necessary in the first place to help the organization of the motor instruments, so that in every successive progress, movement may accompany the intelligence[19].

Montessori gave some valuable suggestions concerning the needs of children at various ages. Although she did not say so explicitly, her observations remind us of her theory of <u>sensitive periods</u>, during which small children can learn certain things better than either before or later in their lives[20]. Following are some extracts from her lecture given in Edinburgh in 1935:

I have found that the child, in his development, passes through certain phases, and the phases in education must correspond with these, so that, instead of dividing the schools into Nursery, Primary, Secondary, University etc., we should divide education according to the planes of individuality[21].

Montessori admitted that her experience had been mainly concerned with the preschool (what we call kindergarten) age of the child:

Those who have followed my method know that I have been taken up largely with the first plane of the child's development, which is from birth to, let us say, six years of age. We find that in this phase the child is passing through a formative period, physiologically formative from the biological point of view ... The child realizes that he can be independent and achieve things through his own efforts ... Now, liberty does not mean to be free to do anything one likes, it is to be able to act without help[22].

Speaking specifically about the elementary school phase, she wrote significantly:

At seven years of age the child changes completely: this may be called the second phase of childhood. Physically the child changes

— for one thing he develops his second teeth, with which he clings to life!

In this phase he moves from concrete to abstract. His independence and aspirations have different goals. He wants to know many things, many things that he cannot actually grasp. I do not say that he becomes a philosopher, but he develops feelings out towards the abstract just as in the first phase he had feelings towards the concrete.

Amongst these things that interest him there is one which must demand our attention. He asks very seriously "What is good and what is bad?" He brings this criterion to bear on the conduct of others, as to whether it is good or bad. If there is religious education, it must be directed towards the absolute and what is good. Before, to love his parents was a necessity; now there is admiration for his parents, for their morality, arising from feelings that his parents are absolutely right. This enables us to give an education in morality which is not less elevated than that given in the secondary schools of today . . . .

The development of culture in the elementary schools is one of the impressive facts that the child has revealed to us . . . The environment may no longer be the house full of small furniture and beautiful things. It is no longer adequate or satisfying.

It is effort that satisfies. The effort he made in the first phase to avoid help, to do things for himself, is no longer enough. He needs a different and a greater effort. Contact with the school is not enough. He needs something different; a more rigid environment with far wider social contacts.

One of the experiments of a social response to these needs of the child is seen in the Scouts . . .

At this stage the child no longer requires an environment on the same model as the previous one, even if more perfect. He needs to go out into the world to make wider contacts. I think this form of exploration has to be used for the cultural development in the school. It is not enough to provide material for the child. It demands to go out into the world and find the material for itself.

> We have provided schools and material; they are not enough, it requires exploration and effort . . .
>
> So we see a new form of world for the second period of childhood, from six to twelve years of age . . . [23]

In view of the lack of more detailed indications regarding the elementary school program, it is interesting to examine Montessori's ideas about what should be taught at the secondary school level (i.e. in the junior and senior high school), for which the elementary school is a preparation. In the Bulletin of the English Montessori Society of Spring 1956 is a long article by Montessori entitled, "The Erdkinder [literally Earth-children]: A scheme for the reform of Secondary Education". Here are some of its main points:

> It is necessary that human personality should be prepared for the unforeseen, not only for the conditions that can be foreseen by prudence and foresight . . . Adaptability — that is the most essential quality; for the progress of the world is continually opening new careers, and at the same time closing or revolutionizing the traditional types of employment[24].

Adaptability, however, should not mean the neglect of cultural subjects or of efforts to develop an all-round personality. Montessori deplored the pressure put on secondary school children to prepare for a career while neglecting to attract their willing cooperation: "They [the children] are [wrongly being] directed by an external and illogical compulsion, and all their best individual energy is wasted . . . [25]"

The program of study, its contents and hours of work should be worked out according to experience:

> It is impossible to fix 'a priori' a detailed program for study and work; we can only give the general plan. This is because a program should only be drawn up gradually and in the light of experience[26].

Order and discipline are essential for the proper exercise of freedom:

> Young people must have enough freedom to allow them to act on individual initiative. But in order that individual action should be free and useful at the same time, it must be restricted within certain limits and rules which give the necessary guidance. These rules and restrictions must be those of the whole institution, not forced on separate individuals as though they had no sense of responsibility and were incapable of conforming of their own free will to necessary regulations. The rules must be just those that are necessary and sufficient to maintain order and ensure progress . . . [27]

A plan of study must be drawn up to ensure that children have clearly defined alternatives from which to choose:

> The environment must make the free choice of occupation easy, and therefore eliminate the waste of time and energy in following vague and uncertain preferences.

> From all this the result will be not only "self-discipline" but a proof that self-discipline is one aspect of individual liberty and the chief factor of success in life[28].

There must not be an overorganization of activities, leaving no time for individual initiative:

> A very important matter is the fundamental "order" in the succession of occupations during the day and the times for the "change-over." This should be experimental at first and develop into an established thing: needs will arise and will have to be dealt with and this will tend to create an organization. But it is necessary to consider not only the active occupations but the need for solitude and quiet, which are essential for the development of the hidden treasures of the soul[29].

As for the "syllabus and methods" recommended for the secondary school, Montessori made the following suggestions:

> The educational syllabus can be drawn up on a general plan which divides it into three:

1. The opening up of ways of expression, which through exercises and external aids will help the development of the personality.

2. The fulfillment of those fundamental needs which we believe to be "formative forces" in the evolution of the soul of man.

3. The theoretical knowledge and practical experience that will make the individual a part of the civilization of the day (General education)[30].

Under the first heading, Montessori suggested "all kinds of artistic occupations open to free choice both as to the time and the nature of the work." There can be individual or group occupations involving "artistic ability and imagination," such as music, practice in the use of language and art, with the stress being on free expression rather than formal teaching.

The second group of subjects should include moral education, mathematics (using special methods of teaching and "plenty of apparatus that demonstrates the materialized abstractions" of math) and the study of foreign languages.

The third group should consist of "the study of the earth, and of living things, that is, geology, geography (including the prehistorical periods), biology, cosmology, zoology, botany, physiology, astronomy, comparative anatomy," as well as "the study of human progress and the building up of civilization in connection with physics and chemistry, mechanics, engineering, and genetics."

The theoretical aspect should alternate with practical work in order to give it a wider application and make it more interesting. The children "should learn to use machines." Montessori added:

These and similar ideas which will awaken a realization of the power of man, and the greatness of civilization should be presented in a form that will stir genuine emotions, for feeling of this kind should exist today together with feelings of religion and patriotism. For in our times science has created a "new world" in which the whole of humanity is bound together by a universal scientific culture[31].

The "Study of the history of mankind" also belongs here, with particular stress on "the history of scientific discoveries and geographical exploration," and the constitution, laws, and customs of the children's own country.

Montessori suggested that this program of education for "Earth-children" should take place preferably in the country, where the students could gradually learn to become independent of their parents, and to adapt themselves to life within a larger society. But an institution of this type cannot be run in chaos and disorder. Hence,

> strict discipline in everything that affects the daily life and the aims
> of the school must be enforced on the staff attached to the school
> as well as on the students, who will only learn to adjust themselves
> to the demands of an ordered environment. This means that the
> staff must take the responsibility for maintaining order until the
> order of voluntary self-discipline is established[32].

Although lacking in detailed instructions about the way the school programs should be implemented, the quotations just presented, nevertheless, show the main guidelines for Montessori education throughout the formative years. They can be summarized as follows:

1. Montessori explained that teachers cannot teach the child directly, because they do not know the interior functioning of its mind, thus teachers can only assist its learning process by supplying the necessary equipment or material.

2. She emphatically affirmed that only the child's spontaneous efforts can succeed in mobilizing the child's entire energy towards the learning activity.

3. In order to ensure the child's all-round development, while preserving its right to choose its work spontaneously, the teacher must make all subjects sufficiently interesting so the child will not wish to limit its activity to a narrow sphere of knowledge while excluding other subjects.

4. To be fully efficient, the child needs to work with its body as well as with its mind. Hence, every mental effort should be accompanied by corresponding physical movements.

5. The child has different needs at different stages of its development, and teaching should take account of this; yet, — as she pointedly remarked — this does not mean the child should be allowed to do everything it wants, only that teachers should help it learn independently: "Liberty is not being free to do anything one likes, it is being able to act without help."

6. On reaching elementary school age, the child changes both physically and mentally, entering a different phase of life. Its mind reaches beyond its immediate environment. It develops abstract ideas, notions of good and bad, and becomes interested in events even in remote parts of the world. It becomes capable of greater intellectual effort and gets satisfaction from doing hard work.

7. During the following (postelementary) phase, the child gradually develops a personality capable of facing the difficulties of life in a changing world. It should learn to be adaptable to various conditions of life. The school program should also take this into account. Montessori was very insistent that children should get as wide a cultural background as possible, but character formation should not be neglected.

8. While keeping their basic right to the choice of work, children should learn to be responsible and to do an orderly piece of work to some reasonable purpose.

9. Children at this stage should learn to live in some wider social grouping, away from their family, where intellectual study would alternate with outdoor physical work.

10. Teachers should see that the child's mind becomes opened to the wonders of scientific discoveries and to the needs of society and the nation, learning about its country, with its laws and its customs, and respecting the established order, not by compulsion, but through gradually acquired self-discipline.

Several writers have commented on the many gaps in the Montessori teaching program. In Orem's symposium on the Montessori method and movement, Martha Kent wrote that "Montessori has no precise method of spelling beyond the dictation of phonetic words and word groups containing the same two- or three-letter phonogram"[33].

Orem himself warned not to expect Montessori to provide the answers to all teaching questions:

> We should be aware of what Dr. Montessori was not offering: an educational method for teaching very young children to read, write and calculate. Maria Montessori observed children from a clinical viewpoint ... to satisfy children's needs from birth through college. Montessori's principles are more the answers of a scientist to the problems of society than the theories of an educator[34].

These words may go too far. Montessori was both a scientist and an eminent educator. Although she left unanswered many questions concerning practical teaching, she left no doubt about the general spirit in which education should be carried on, at whatever stage.

No educator was more insistent than Montessori in pointing out that at all learning levels it is the child's own eagerness to learn that is the most important thing that should be nurtured and maintained. This is because what it retains from its learning is far less important than the process of learning itself, as it is the latter that forms the child's character, and "builds the man." It is the educators' prime task to find ways to arouse the child's interest in whatever subject they want it to learn, so that the child can put its whole heart into the work, learning better in a shorter time as a result.

One of the chief characteristics of the Montessori method and one she was proud to point out, is the economy of effort and time from the social point of view, as a result of children's spontaneous work. In an article in the Rivista Montessori she wrote that a skillful teacher does not mind having 40, 60, or even 80 children of varying ages and attainment levels. She said because the children learn faster this way and fewer teachers are needed, this method is very economical[35]. I myself believe — with due respect to Maria Montessori — that many teachers would protest against having so many children in a class and would say that a class of 20 to 25 is sufficient, especially at the elementary level — but then Montessori was never a teacher herself in sole charge of a class, only a researcher-consultant. Some remarkable results have been achieved by very talented teachers in handling classes of 40 or more children, but the possibilities for an average teacher must not be overrated.

The question of movement accompanying mental work needs some qualification. Is a child writing an essay moving sufficiently by using its pencil? Or when reading a book, where only its eyeballs are moving? And when a teacher is giving a lesson, however short, should the children be encouraged or not to shuffle their feet, walk around, or roll on the carpet? Fortunately, we see that as children grow older, their brains become capable of working without being stimulated by movement, and sometimes they require complete immobility for proper concentration (e.g. when playing chess and examining a difficult position). But the fact remains that a lot of indulgence is needed with "fidgety" children, particularly when they have to make mental efforts of which they are not too fond. The same is, after all, equally the case with adults who smoke or doodle and sometimes fall asleep when their mental effort is not connected with physical activity. I have often envied my female colleagues who were able to do some knitting during tedious staff meetings. I thought I could have paid attention to the proceedings much better if I had had something to do with my hands.

As in many other instances, the problem, in practice, has to be solved by the teacher's common sense, according to the circumstances and the possibilities available at the time. Some deviation from a principle, forced by the circumstances, does not mean one has abandoned the method and that the teaching is not Montessori any more. It is significant that despite her idealism, Montessori was always a very practical person. She would be adamant in letting an eagerly working child follow its inner impulse and study at its own pace. But she would stand no nonsense if a child was disturbing others or causing damage to itself or the environment.

In The Montessori Method, at pp. 87/88, she wrote:

> If any educational act is to be efficacious, it will be only that which tends to HELP toward the complete unfolding of [the child's] life.

To be thus helpful it is necessary rigorously to avoid the ARREST OF SPONTANEOUS MOVEMENTS AND THE IMPOSITION OF ARBITRARY TASKS. It is of course understood that here we do not speak of useless or dangerous acts, for these must be SUPPRESSED, DESTROYED . . .

And at page 92 she continued thus:

I saw children with their feet on the tables, or with their fingers in their noses, and no intervention was made to correct them. I saw others push their companions, and I saw dawn in the faces of these an expression of violence; and not the slightest attention on the part of the teacher. Then I had to intervene to show with what absolute rigor it is necessary to hinder, and little by little suppress, all those things which we must not do, so that the child may come to discern clearly between good and evil. And all this because our aim is to discipline FOR ACTIVITY, FOR WORK, FOR GOOD; not for IMMOBILITY, not for PASSIVITY, not for OBEDIENCE.

It is illuminating to read in these passages Montessori's observations about the changes occurring in the child at the end of the preschool period and the need of a different teaching approach after that age. The child's awakening moral sense has to be cultivated, its widening interests developed, and its growing feeling of belonging to both the visible and invisible society supported and encouraged. New materials and new methods are obviously needed that can stimulate "exploration and effort."

The entire post-preschool period — which is the object of this study — must, according to Montessori, form a preparation for the following adolescent stage. Adolescent school programs should not exclusively aim at the individual's future bread-winning capacity, but should go beyond it to develop the whole person. And although the "education must be wide and very thorough," the child's personality must be allowed to develop. It follows that already at the preceding elementary stage the child must be helped to develop all its mental, physical, and moral potentialities.

Forcing the child into an imposed program is a "waste of time," while liberty leading to self-discipline must be preserved as a "chief factor of success in life." All the same, Montessori said that eventually the child must be brought to follow a certain "order" in its occupations, although this has to be done "experimentally at first," in a way the child will willingly accept. The subjects studied should include training in artistic and linguistic expression and the study of the earth's past, present, and foreseeable future. Thus, the environment widens to embrace the whole universe, and the study of mathematics becomes necessary as a clue to an understanding of it.

In the moral field, Montessori wanted the child to learn to live within society and to be able to adapt itself to it. Children therefore have to be taught to respect and follow "the demands of an ordered environment." Hence, the staff in charge of the "Earth-children" must enforce "strict discipline in everything that affects the daily life and the aims of the school," until such time as voluntary self-discipline makes harsh measures unnecessary.

An analysis of Montessori's educational theories shows there are a great number of possible variations in applying her method in both the elementary and high school within the framework of her basic principles. Unlike in the preschool (2½ to 5 years), we find in Montessori's writings no fixed school program for the later years, no detailed description of ways in which the teacher is to proceed for the following 10 years to help children educate themselves as the system requires. Some schools — such as the Gatehouse Learning Center — have already started to carry the Montessori method into the teenage phase and even further. But are they merely pursuing the path indicated by Montessori or are they building a program of their own that in their opinion Montessori would have approved? A few devices for math and language study worked out by Montessori and her followers do not constitute a school program, so the gaps have to be filled somehow, and the field is open to individual attempts and interpretations of Montessori's ideas. We need to know whether the practices Montessori did not personally test are universally successful, whether there are no better materials or methods, and to what extent we may depart from the established routine in other ways. We must learn what to do when we run into difficulties, how to behave in certain situations, how to avoid making mistakes and gradually sinking into the daily routine of the old school ways we were trying to avoid. Above all, there are a few fundamental questions to be answered if we are to be sure we are not straying from the principles Montessori laid down and that we have decided to follow. Let us examine some of the more important ones.

In all educational theories, including the Montessori method, there is a fundamental dilemma, an opposition of two principles: spontaneous activity against programming, and creativity against structure.

Even in the preschool Montessori class there is a program, an order in which different sets of apparatus are to be demonstrated. Apart from the exercises in practical life, which the children love because they see their mothers doing them at home, there are exercises for acquiring control over the fingers, sensorial exercises, exercises for developing the skills of writing and reading and using numbers. The child does not spontaneously ask for the writing and reading materials, but the educator puts them in the environment because he thinks it is good for the child to know how to read and write.

There are many things we want the child to learn at the elementary school age, too, and we have to see that it learns them in order to reach the standard required by the country's educational authorities. Montessori wanted the children to learn even more than in the conventional schools, but she wanted the teacher to observe and find out at what stage they may become interested in particular subjects or topics and how their interest can be aroused. She wanted children to learn as much as possible, with the minimum of pressure, if any. But as far as concrete detailed ways of teaching are concerned, she offered very little help for the implementation of the elementary program, and even less for the high school stage. Montessori was well aware of this, and was willing to accept into her method any genuine contribution to helping the child's development, as long as it is based on a scientifically worked out environment.

She expressed her feelings and convictions on the subject in an article in the Rivista Montessori of March/April 1932, where she defined the aim of the magazine (in my translation from Italian):

> Above all we must be aware of the object of this magazine: we understand that object to be a "contribution to the real building of a new civilized world."

> Our contribution is not a system of ideas, but a true and proper "reconstruction" that starts with the education of children and the

practical organization of an environment for development which has given spectacular results . . . .

If this is its object, the magazine can be called MONTESSORI, since, as many people are saying, this is "a common name," which signifies in short a whole complex of clear and definite actions and ideas of educational and social character . . . .

We are one-sided and militant, but we admit to having allies, with whom we want to fight side by side, recognizing them as comrades and fighters for the same goal.

She expressed herself still more precisely in her talks to reporters from some Spanish papers, reproduced in the "Montessori Notes" of July/August 1934:

People talk much about the Montessori "Method" . . . but I must tell you it is not exactly a method — that is the name applied by the Americans to our system in their desire to simplify things. That which I have divulged is on the whole a conjunction of observations obtained from having devoted myself for many years to studying both the body and soul of children.

And very significantly she added:

Before many years have gone by, the teachers of primary education will be interested solely in these methods. Today, I have the satisfaction of knowing that not only the "nurses," but the professors of advanced studies, are applying them.

All this . . . has not been done by me alone, but thanks also to the collaboration of others in all parts of the world.

These words show quite clearly that Montessori had no intention of presenting a precise and crystallized system of education, but considered herself rather as the leader of a movement in which many people are encouraged to participate, a movement in which the decisive factor was scientific experiment and observation.

It is hardly surprising, however, that in an educational movement of such magnitude, extending the world over, there are tendencies to monopolize the teaching and claim that such-and-such educational materials and practices are the only ones to be called Montessori, to the exclusion of others. I call them errors of judgment. In my view, there are three main misconceptions that fall into this category. They have to be fought off at all costs if the integrity and greatness of the Montessori ideals are to be preserved for future generations.

The first misconception is that every part of the system must be either have been conceived or recommended by Montessori herself. We have seen from the quotations presented here and those in chapter 1 that Montessori did not consider her contribution to be purely a personal matter, but a collective work to be based on experience and scientific exploration by many people with the same purpose as the one she had in mind. By implication, applying the same principle, Montessori submitted her own contribution to the criterion of scientific inquiry. If any materials or other teaching devices invented or recommended by Montessori should prove ineffective, outdated, or less successful than others, they should be discarded and replaced by others more suitable for bringing about the full development and independence of the child[36].

A second misconception is that Montessori schools should use materials and methods different from other schools, and show in every aspect something original, not seen anywhere else. This shows a complete misunderstanding of the basic ideas and aims of the system. Are we to give priority to originality over the benefit to the child? If other schools, other educational thinkers, approach the Montessori line, we should support them, correct them if necessary, but learn from them if they can teach us something conforming better to the Montessori goals. If the materials of Cuisenaire, Unifix, Stern, or Dienes are better at some stage than Montessori beads and counting boards, it would be an injury to the children not to adopt them. The same goes for other subjects, reading and writing methods, history and geography projects, experimental science, and so on.

Third, some Montessori teachers and principals have an unjustified prejudice against the use of textbooks. It is true that few textbooks are written for the direct use of the child, for working independently, with only occasional help of the teacher, and even those that are meant for individual   work   often   prove   insufficiently   tested   against misunderstanding.   But basically, there is no difference between a textbook and a collection of sets of loose-leaf cards painstakingly written by the teacher — except that the latter are likely to become less presentable after frequent use, and more likely to be discarded if they do not meet the teacher's expectations.   Many textbooks are published in loose-leaf form.   But this does not seem to be practical, at least at the elementary or high school levels, when children are more mature and want to see some target to be reached, and a certain continuity and order in the subject they are studying.   Besides, loose leaves are apt to get lost or damaged.

Many current textbooks published are the work of teams of experienced teachers, and undergo considerable testing before publication.   At the elementary school stage, when children are able to read fluently, it is unreasonable and educationally wrong to deprive them of the use of such excellent manuals or workbooks.   Besides, there is a great value in the attractiveness of illustrations and binding of modern textbooks.   According to the fourth principle for Montessori materials suggested in the previous chapter, they should be attractive as well as serviceable in other aspects.   I have often found a remarkable improvement in children's performance from the moment they received attractive workbooks with which to work. Even if the workbooks contain mistakes, it is easier to correct them than to write a new book of equal excellence.

Having decided on the materials and textbooks for children, the next step is to find the delicate balance between planning and freedom of work at the child's own choice and pace, between structure and creation, spontaneity and pressure.   This is a thing schools and teachers have to decide for themselves, using tact, intuition, and common sense, and based on circumstances.

One way of resolving this problem has been adopted by the Dalton Plan, which was said to have been inspired by Montessori.   In this plan, children do not have to sit in classes, all working on the same subject at the same time.   Instead, each child decides by itself which subject to choose at any given time, and goes to the corresponding classroom where the specialist teacher awaits, ready to help if the need arises.

In the Gatehouse Learning Center in London, run on Montessori lines for children from 2½ to 18, every child in the senior school follows an individual plan of study with a list of subjects on which to work, and has to spend a specified number of 30-minute periods on each subject during the week. Teachers sign student attendance cards, and the school's form master or mistress checks the daily performance of each child at the end of the morning. No marks are given, but the names of children who have distinguished themselves by a particularly good effort are read aloud at the daily assembly the following morning.

Children seem to like this system because of the freedom it gives them to organize their time and the opportunity for moving from one room to another, instead of sitting for long hours in the same place. This system also offers each child individual attention whenever difficulty arises. It is a fairly strenuous system for teachers because at any given time children of different ability and using different books or teaching aids are working in the same classroom, and teachers must keep records of student progress. These difficulties, however, are amply compensated by the pleasant, unrestrained atmosphere of the classroom and the cooperative attitude of the children.

Each child is allowed to work at its own pace, according to its ability and interest in the subject. No one is forced to go faster than ability allows, and no one is held back because others are proceeding at a slower pace.

At the end of the term, every teacher writes a report on each child in their care. In line with Montessori's principles, great care is taken to express the report in a positive way, to be encouraging, not depressing, emphasizing the child's good points and efforts rather than listing faults or shortcomings.

Children have the opportunity to express their opinions on school matters in a monthly general assembly. They may praise or criticize the teachers, but every criticism must be accompanied by a positive suggestion that indicates how things could be improved.

One of the characteristics of the Gatehouse School is that it accepts a certain proportion of handicapped and disabled children who may be dyslexic, emotionally disturbed, even blind, brain-damaged, or suffering from cerebral palsy or Down syndrome. Normal children are encouraged to help their less fortunate comrades in their study, in moving about and doing various jobs. The moral effect of such cooperation is considerable, and both the able-bodied and the disabled profit from this daily contact.

This brings us to another point. To be true to the spirit of Montessori education it should be remembered that progress in academic matters is only one side of normalization, and that it must be a reflection of the formation of character. It is, therefore, of paramount importance to care about the children's hearts as well as their brains. Talks about matters concerning the school as a whole, the town, the nation, and the world; discussions about social problems; and encouragement in giving help to the poor, lonely, and disabled should be regular features of school life.

Independently of all the skills and knowledge children may acquire, one of the most important things they learn is the art of living together, working together, playing happily and talking about topics of common interest with each other, tolerating each other's faults and making the best of the other person's qualities; in short, becoming good and acceptable friends and companions, reliable workers, and active participants in collective life. The schedule of activities in the classroom should allow ample opportunity for communication between children both at work and at play. They should have time for the spontaneous organization of games, plays, literary or artistic productions, with the minimum of interference from adults, unless they expressly ask for their advice and help. It is not possible to determine in advance the amount of time to be allocated for such purposes — spontaneous outbursts may occur unexpectedly and fade out equally quickly. But the art of leadership required for a collective activity is so rare and precious that when it does manifest itself in young children it deserves every support and consideration, as long as it is directed to a good purpose. Schools in which the whole time is structured so that children have little time for talking and free movement do not prepare them properly for future life in society. Children who have not been integrated into their miniature society at an early age will probably continue living their own private lives without caring for the community when they grow up. The results of this are broken marriages; dissension between brothers and sisters; workers caring only about money, without devotion to the work they are doing; employers and politicians indifferent to the well-being of their employees and the people they represent; and so on. It can be assumed that children's general behavior and attitudes to the school will later be reflected in their relationships to society. Yet patterns of behavior cannot be instilled by oral exhortations, but must be worked out in practical life. It is during these noisy and seemingly wasteful times, when the children are free to pursue their self-motivated activities, that personalities are built and the foundations are laid for the society of the future.

Naturally, there are problems involved in putting a Montessori education program into operation. In the following chapters, I put forward some suggestions for implementing elementary and high school education along truly Montessori lines (although conditions will naturally differ in various parts of the country, and every school and every teacher has to decide which propositions can be accepted in their plan of work).

4

Freedom and Discipline

Freedom and discipline pose a problem of which every teacher and parent is well aware. Teachers never like to admit they have disciplinary problems with children, even when talking informally with each other. An inability to curb students is considered a weakness on their part, and a major flaw in their reputation of job fitness. Yet, it would be better if teachers did talk more about these two issues, discuss them and try to help one another. Besides, trying to hide their difficulties often leads them to exercise more pressure than necessary and makes them irritable, with adverse effects on both themselves and the children.

Obviously there must be some discipline, in order to avoid chaos. Chaos prevents teachers from doing what they want, hence it limits freedom. Teachers become enslaved by the obstacles to their actions, by the lack of order and control of the situation. Children feel it too, and they themselves sometimes beg teachers to "make silence" or to stop those who are misbehaving and making work and concentration impossible. The problem is how to balance freedom against discipline, without having the latter unduly infringing the former.

Unfortunately, this is a topic on which Montessori gave some theoretical advice, but little in the way of practical direction:

> When the child is greatly absorbed in its work, the teacher must respect its concentration and must not interfere either to correct or to encourage. This is the time when the principle of "non-intervention" must be most strictly observed. Certain teachers have assimilated this principle in a superficial way; they told themselves that all they had to do was to distribute the material and to retire, no matter what happened. This resulted in terrible disorder in their school, because the respect for a child's activity which is expressed by non-intervention applies only when some

Rapt concentration in fitting the cylinders into the right holes (also see photo facing page 117). Photo: Nienhuis Montessori, Zelhem, Holland.

Learning numbers and matching counters to each one. Photo: Caroline Hardy, Gatehouse School, London.

interesting phenomenon manifests itself in the child's life; but it has no place when its attention is dissipated in the midst of complete disorder. I have seen disruptive children who used all sorts of material in a completely wrong way; the teacher walked by like a sphinx, in complete silence. Such was the mistaken behavior of the teacher who was afraid of disturbing the disorder, while she ought to have feared only to disturb orderly behavior[37].

See also the following significant passages in "The Montessori Method":

The first dawning of real discipline comes through work. At a given moment it happens that a child becomes keenly interested in a piece of work, showing it by the expression of its face, by its intense attention, by its perseverance in the same exercise. That child has set foot upon the road to discipline. . . .

Once the habit of work is formed, we must supervise it with scrupulous accuracy, graduating the exercises as experience has taught us. In our effort to establish discipline, we must rigorously apply the principles of the method. It is not to be obtained by words; no-one learns self-discipline "through hearing another man speak." The phenomenon of discipline needs as preparation a series of complete actions, such as are presupposed in the genuine application of a really educative method. Discipline is always reached by indirect means. The end is obtained, not by attacking the mistake and fighting it, but by developing activity in spontaneous work [page 350].

At times she seemed to take the side of the children. In the "Secret of Childhood" she wrote:

The naughtiness and disobedience of the child are the expression of a vital conflict between his creative urge and his love for the adult who does not understand it. When instead of obedience the adult encounters temper, he should always attribute it to this conflict, and to the defense of a vital element necessary to the child's growth[38].

Montessori said that self-discipline appears when children are normalized — which sounds like a tautology — but she did not say precisely how to maintain discipline before normalization. Should a child be punished who is uncooperative and obstructive? If so, when and how should punishment be inflicted, and to what limits can teachers go? Should teachers demand strict obedience, with punishment as an alternative, until the child becomes normalized and learns to discipline itself?

The answers to some of these questions have already been discussed — yet others are more difficult to solve. But on a correct answer to them depends the whole difference between a Montessori school and a conventional one; and if we believe in Montessori's educational principles we must be quite clear as to whether our actions are in agreement with her ideology.

To achieve self-discipline children must be given some freedom of action, — otherwise they have little incentive to discipline themselves, or even no chance to take any initiative; all they have left is the freedom to obey.

Montessori rightly mocked people who consider obedience as the supreme virtue in children. She wrote in the Rivista Montessori:

> The child who has never learnt to do things by itself, to control its actions, to master its own will, later turns into an adult who is easily led and who needs the support of other people.
>
> A schoolchild that is constantly discouraged and repressed acquires that combination of anxiety and a lack of self-confidence which is called shyness: which is found later in an adult prone to discouragement and submissiveness, incapable of moral resistance. Obedience to which the child is subjected in the family and at school, obedience without reason or justice, creates an adult who easily surrenders to fate: that punishment, so widespread in schools, of exposing the weak child to public rebukes almost equivalent to the ordeal of the pillory, creates in its mind an unreasonable fear of public opinion, even if it is unjust and evidently mistaken. And among these and many other adjustments which lead to a permanent condition of inferiority, stands out the attitude of devotion, almost worship, for leaders who represent for the beguiled man a father or a teacher, personalities who were imposed on the child as perfect and infallible. In such a way discipline becomes synonymous with enslavement[39].

On the other hand, Montessori showed no sympathy for the child who is obviously disruptive, and she recognized that teachers must be "firm." In the "Advanced Method," she warned that some children do not respond immediately to the stimulus of the material, with the resulting disorder:

> when the mistress makes a kind of chain of that "liberty" she is to respect, and a dogma of the correlation existing between the stimulus and the childish soul. Experienced teachers on the other hand, understand better that LIBERTY begins when the LIFE that must be developed in the child is initiated[40].

Therefore, there are two seemingly contradictory postulates: There must be order and discipline, yet it should not be enforced. There must be obedience, yet without abolishing the freedom to transgress.

In the light of the general principles of the method, the solution to this apparent contradiction is as follows: Self-discipline must grow as a part of the general development and maturity of the child. Those who say that we must keep punishing the child for its transgressions until it becomes normalized, fail to understand the basic psychological truth that self-discipline must be motivated from within. As long as the chief motivation for good behavior is the desire to avoid punishment, the child feels free to disobey as soon as the threat of punishment recedes, and the inner motivation hardly comes into play.

Montessori maintained that self-discipline is a part of the general spiritual health of the child, just as the normal function of each organ flows from the physical health of the whole body. Hence, when the child is placed in the right environment, when both its mind and its body find all the occupations it needs, disobedience ceases to have any point, and disappears. The main thing, therefore, is to give the child interesting work that it loves doing. Then it will give no more trouble.

In "The Montessori Method" she wrote:

> To obtain discipline, it is quite useless to count on reprimands or spoken exhortations. Such means might perhaps at the beginning have an appearance of efficacy, but after a while cease to have any effect. Experience shows that the first dawning of real discipline comes through work. At a given moment it happens that a child becomes keenly interested in a piece of work, showing it by the

expression of his face, by his intense attention, by his perseverance in the same exercise.

Once the habit of work is formed, we must supervise it with scrupulous accuracy, graduating the exercises as experience has taught us. In our effort to establish discipline, we must rigorously apply the principles of the method. It is not to be obtained by words; no man learns self-discipline "through hearing another man speak." The phenomenon of discipline needs as preparation a series of complete actions, such as are presupposed in the genuine application of a really educative method. Discipline is reached always by indirect means. The end is obtained, not by attacking the mistake and fighting it, but by developing activity in spontaneous work[41].

At the end of the book, Montessori repeated this most fundamental of her principles:

These are the first outlines of an experiment which shows a form of indirect discipline in which there is substituted for the critical and sermonizing teacher a rational organization of work and of liberty for the child. It involves a conception of life more usual in religious fields than in those of academic pedagogy, in as much as it has recourse to the spiritual energies of mankind, but it is founded on work and on liberty which are the two paths to all civic progress[42].

And again, as if trying to put a seal on this "conception of life" of hers, she remarked:

Truly our social life is too often only the darkening and the death of the natural life that is in us. These methods tend to guard that spiritual fire within man, to keep his real nature unspoiled and to set it free from the oppressive and degrading yoke of society[43].

In practice, of course, things are not that simple. Children are human beings, not angels, and besides, in every school there are some students who never had early training in a Montessori preschool. Such individuals carry in them rebellious feelings toward teachers and a hesitant attitude acquired in conventional public or private schools, where, in the opinion of most students, working for work's sake is silly, and opposition to the teacher's directives is an act of heroism and a proof of toughness. Some of these children can have a very disruptive influence on their schoolmates, and it may be difficult to normalize them in the ordinary way. The attention they get as a result of their misbehavior is their reward, and for that reason a special technique is required to restrain them or at least prevent their harmful influence on the class.

Positive measures should be discussed. Sylvia Ashton-Warner, whose teacher's genius is 100% Montessorian without her professing it, said in her inspiring book Teacher, that many educational troubles seem to spring from suppression of the child's urge for creativity. She wrote that: "So often I have seen the destructive vent, beneath an onslaught of creativity, dry up under my eyes"[44].

Speaking of New Zealand people, as can also be said of every modern civilized society, she called them a "body of people with their inner resources atrophied," and added:

> Everything, from material requirements to ideas, is available ready-made. From mechanical gadgets in the shops to sensation in the films, they can buy almost anything they fancy. They can buy life itself from the film and radio — canned life. . . . [45]

Yet this did not mar her optimism, even though the prevailing state of affairs may carry the danger of war:

> True, the toyshops are full of guns . . . the blackboards, clayboards and easels burst with war play. But I am unalarmed. My concern is the rearing of the creative disposition, for creativity . . . must in the end defy, if not defeat, the capacity for destruction . . . For as Enrich Fromm says, "The amount of destructiveness in a child is proportionate to the amount to which the expansiveness of his life has been curtailed. Destructiveness is the outcome of the unlived life"[46].

There can be no doubt about the validity of the foregoing remarks, against those who consider any activity outside the school program as a "waste of time." Creativity is the first step to normalization, and if a child is seriously occupied with some creation of its own, whether it be work with teaching material or an airplane made of improvised scraps of paper and plastic, the general Montessori principle applies: Don't interfere. But simulated creative activity may sometimes be a mere escape from doing schoolwork or attending a lesson. Such cases must be left to the discretion and tact of the teacher.

Let us however not beat about the bush, and admit that there are cases, especially at the beginning of the school year, before the children get into the habit of "being good," when a quick and decisive punishment is necessary. But let us be careful: It applies only if it is likely to be effective (i.e. if its educational purpose is likely to be achieved).

If the punishment causes resentment, humiliation, and discouragement in the child, if it engenders hostility toward the teacher, or if, as often happens, it gives the child a sense of achievement, a victory over the exasperated teacher and aggrandizement in the eyes of his schoolmates, its educational purpose will be missed, and the transgression will likely recur, bringing with it more trouble for the teacher.

Rudolf Dreikurs, in his book entitled <u>Children, the Challenge</u>[47], provided some good, sound, and very Montessori-like advice on the subject, quoting many examples from home and school experience. He saw three main sources of disorderly actions by children, each requiring a different remedy. They are a desire for undue attention, a wish to dominate the adult, and a feeling of inferiority that results in abandoning all effort for initiative and cooperation.

Starting with the first point: If a child screams without apparent reason or deliberately causes some disorder such as scattering things about or upsetting another child at work, it would be wrong to make a scene, to rebuke the child sharply in front of others, send it out of the room, causing it to resist, and so forth, because this is exactly what the unruly child wants. The child will repeat the behavior to obtain the same treatment. The other children will look at the disruptive child, some will admire its boldness, wishing they had the nerve to do the same, and so forth. The child will become a hero. The teacher might guess the reason for this sudden desire for attention and try to react accordingly. Perhaps the child is bored, frustrated at not finding anything interesting to do, feels jealous because the teacher has been spending time with another child, or has experienced some emotional upset at home (e.g. quarrels between parents, mother's illness, birth of another baby, etc.). It is clearly impossible to reflect on such possibilities at the time, but it may indicate a line of action for the future. In the meantime, it is best not to give the child the attention it wants, but to ignore it, pretending one is too busy to notice that anything wrong has occurred. Alternatively, disapproval can be shown in a calm tone, with the teacher continuing his work until the outburst stops and the child becomes ready to accept a positive suggestion: "Would you like to pick up these things with me?" or "Will you check Billy's sums with the answer book?" If stronger measures are needed, the child should be spoken to in a low voice, so as to attract as little of the other children's attention as possible.

Some more practical advice from Dreikurs included never asking a whole group of children if they know "Who did it?" but rather letting the whole group suffer as the consequence of a misdeed of some of its members, which has been at least tolerated, if not encouraged, by the others (e.g. tell them to clean up a mess they have made) — for in most cases they are in effect all in the same conspiracy.

Regarding the second source of disorderliness, it is usually the teacher's fault if he gets involved in a power struggle with the child. "Get out!" "Come here at once!" "Will you pick it up immediately!" — phrases such as these, spoken in a raised voice and commanding tone hurt the child's dignity and provoke it to show opposition. The teacher must not let himself be dominated by the child, but he must refrain from showing a taste for power by demanding blind and immediate obedience, and expecting the child to accept harsh and insulting words the teacher would not tolerate from the child himself.

In the third case, a child may show apathy and refuse to do the work by itself, repeating "I can't do these sums, solve these problems, understand these directions; you must stay here and help me!" when the teacher's attention is needed elsewhere. In this case the policy should be not to withdraw all help, but to give the child an easier book or suggest it should work with another child, so as to increase its self-confidence and prove to it that it can indeed do a lot of work without being helped.

In the case of a deliberate and repeated breaking of rules, some showdown may be needed to prevent a general slackness or to protect children from being bullied, teased, or disturbed by undisciplined individuals. The general principle in such cases is not to raise one's voice, but to make the rules and the consequence of their breaking clear in advance, and be firm in applying these provisions consistently, without further argument. Better still, the need for such decisions can be discussed in a meeting with the children and they can accept them, so that the sanctions do not appear to be the teacher's arbitrary rules, and the transgressors cease to have a valid excuse for their behavior. The best course is to have a logical connection between the transgression and its consequence. If a child soils its desk with a magic marker, the marker should be taken away from it, and the child should be asked to clean up the desk before starting another occupation. If the child disturbs the peace by running across the room and shouting, it should be made to stand still by the wall until it calms down and can remain quiet. If the child persistently disturbs others at work by talking, it should be made to move its desk away from its friends or go outside the room. In other words, the child should be made aware of the consequences of its actions — not as an act of retribution or vengeance, nor as humiliation, but as protection of the others. The transgressor should always be given the alternative of either obeying voluntarily or being forced to it, and it should be told that it may return (or have a confiscated object returned, as the case may be) as soon as it feels it can cooperate.

There will be cases when parents have to be asked to withdraw the child from the school, to protect the group, when all efforts have failed to obtain the child's co-operation. To prevent a loss of income for the school, the administration should ensure there is always a waiting list of entrance candidates. New entrants not having good records from previous schools should be given a trial period of 2 or 3 months before being accepted for the whole year. However, some children need a long time before they adapt themselves, and it is a great joy for a teacher to see the recovery of a difficult child, which may come quite unexpectedly, for reasons unknown. The removal of a child from the school may also have negative effects both on the child removed and on other members of the group who may have liked the child as a friend and companion.

It is important to "make peace" with the child concerned after a conflict. The teacher should talk to the child when it has calmed down, make the child admit that the measure taken was just, and also apologize for his loss of temper. Reconciliation is always easy and pleasant, for children rarely hold grudges for long. Often youngsters fight in a rage with each other, and an hour later are to be found happily playing together. It is different with adults. A teacher may feel uneasy with the child after a conflict, and this will be felt by the child. The child may feel unliked by the teacher, and the strained relations may persist for some time. A quiet word of explanation may restore friendship, which is the basis of all discipline.

Dealing with hyperactive children may be the most difficult situation. Such children often have very short spans of concentration and may keep moving from one desk to another, shouting, moving furniture and materials, and disturbing everyone around. These children need a lot of manual occupation, such as sweeping and cleaning or construction with bricks or other materials. It is even difficult to make them finish whatever work they have started. A remedy may be found by letting such children work in association with one or two others. Working associations may develop quite spontaneously, and successfully, among friends. I have seen children working happily together at a jigsaw puzzle or painting, where each of them did their bit, discussing details with their partner and producing quite a satisfactory result in the end. In such cases, noise resulting from a conversation between partners may cause some disturbance, but it may be worth tolerating in order to get some work done by an individual who otherwise would stay idle.

Many problems are solved by the passing of time, through gradual maturing and physiological changes. It often amazes me to see how much children change both physically and mentally in a single year. On the other hand, it must be remembered that the normalization process does not proceed uniformly. There are ups and downs and regressions; progress in one direction need not be followed by advance in others. First of all, learning in children is not a continuous process. As H.R. Kohl rightly remarked: "Children's learning is EPISODIC rather than vertical or linear. One can think of it as a spider's web rather than as a staircase"[48].

The same applies to character development. Even though the learning and behavior processes seem to be interconnected, there are bound to be periods of stagnation and regression either on the academic side or on the social one, for reasons that are not always clear.

A major problem in all schools, whether traditional or modern, is noise. In conventional schools, where antagonism between teacher and students is a chronic malaise, the prevention of noise is a basic condition for keeping control of the class. A teacher who fails to stop the first murmur that reaches his ears will soon find the noise rising and spreading; the children, for whom immobility of body is a torture, will ascribe the teacher's indulgence to weakness; they will start playing him up, and unless he quickly resorts to drastic measures, he will start having an endless struggle on his hands. The children will always try to take as much liberty as they can, and the teacher will constantly have to restrain them. This is mainly why the teacher's job is so exhausting and many teachers end by becoming nervous wrecks, despite their long vacations.

In Montessori schools, the problem is even more difficult, although in the end more rewarding. As children of different levels work in the same classroom, often at different subjects, too, the teacher has to coach them individually, bending over them and helping them, so that watching the group to prevent any unauthorized word or movement becomes impossible. Anyway, in most Montessori schools children are allowed to walk about and talk to each other, like in an office or club. Teachers cannot check whether their talk concerns the work they are doing or yesterday's TV show; they cannot prevent occasional laughter, and they would not want it either, for teachers want children to be happy and relaxed.

In these conditions, it is essential that the children should have some work to do in which they are interested, and that they consider the teacher as a friend, not a jailer. Otherwise, there would be permanent chaos. But even when everyone is busy working, children in their near teens can have quite loud voices, and are fond of using them. There will be occasionally a loud call: "Give me back those scissors!" "Holly, come here!" "Don't do that!" and so on, and in growing excitement it soon becomes difficult to concentrate. What is the teacher to do?

In the first place, one must admit that when 20 to 30 young people work in one room, a certain amount of undesirable noise is unavoidable. Suppressing noise by shouting "Silence!" or "Shhhhhh!" is not much good as its effect will soon wear off, and no one will take any more notice.

But noise in a free school is not necessarily synonymous with indiscipline. As Ashton-Warner observed: "Noise, noise, noise, yes. But if you don't like noise, don't be a teacher. Because children are noisy animals[49].

And in another place: "Of course there is a lot of noise, but there's a lot of work too."[50]

And again: "The noise doesn't matter. The children writing are just about as talkative as the others. But I let it be like that. Suppression is the last thing in organic work."[51]

And how true are the words of this amazingly successful teacher, when she wistfully admitted:

> For long sitting, watching and pondering (all so unprofessional), I have found out the worst enemies to what we call teaching. There are two.

> The first is the children's interest in each other. It plays the very devil with orthodox methods. If only they'd stop talking to each other, playing with each other, fighting with each other and loving each other. This unseemly and unlawful communication! In self-defense I've got to use the damn thing. So I harness the communication, since I can't control it, and base my method on it. They read in pairs, sentence and sentence about. There's no time for either to get bored. . . . They teach each other all their work in pairs . . . arguing with, correcting, abusing or smiling at each other. And between them all the time is togetherness, so that learning is so mixed up with relationship that it becomes part of it. What an unsung creative medium is relationship!

> The other trouble . . . is their desire to make things. If only they'd sit . . . with their hands still and wait until they're told to do something and told how to do it. The way they draw bombers and make them with anything and roar around the room with them[52].

But in spite of all this, she does have control of the class. She quotes her inspector as saying, "Discipline is a matter of being able to get attention when you want it."[53]

Based on this principle, she wrote:

> I'm still learning how to let it fly and yet to discipline it. It's got to be disciplined in a way that's hard to say. It still must have its range and its wing, ... it must still be free to dare the gale and sing, but it's got to come home at the right time and next at the right place. For the spirit to live its freest, the mind must acknowledge discipline. ... They've got to listen to me when I speak and obey what I speak. I can only say that I don't often speak. And that I carefully weigh what I do speak. But the track between these two conditions, the spiritual freedom and the outer discipline, is narrower than any tightrope, and seldom can I say that I have walked it[54].

So here is another conflicting duality: How much noise is one to allow, without impairing enthusiasm and spontaneity?

As with the recommendations concerning how to counter disorder and chaos, the remedy here is still free, spontaneous work. Hence, getting the children absorbed in work of their choice must take precedence over anything else. But spontaneity in work cannot stand alone. It needs to be both fed and limited by teaching, which means some direction, and program. Both freedom and its limitations must result from the school program. How to apportion one against the other depends on the circumstances and the discretion of the teacher. In ideal conditions, there should be ample space and a large volume of air between the floor and the ceiling, allowing the noise to spread out without becoming oppressive. But in schools with limited possibilities, where children are obliged to work in small, crowded rooms, liberty has to be restricted to protect everyone's peace and nerves. The character and temperament of the teachers concerned must also be taken into account. Those who cannot tolerate noise will have to see that the children are quieter by appropriate organization of study, order of work, time of breaks, and persuasion.

The noise problem is discussed again later.

In cases of collective misbehavior, it must be stressed that neither individuals nor a group can be expected to change behavior patterns all at once. If they do, possibly as a result of a threat or severe punishment, the change is bound to be artificial and shaky. When children are taught an academic subject, they are not expected to retain more than a few pages at a time, and teachers make allowances for some of the matter to be forgotten after a while, and old mistakes to be repeated before the new knowledge takes root. In the same way, when children are taught the rules of good behavior, only gradual progress can be achieved, by trying to inculcate one single rule at a time. When children get into the habit of observing it, the teacher can start teaching the next one, and so on.

The foregoing rule must be remembered in those cases — not infrequent — when a Montessori teacher is put in charge of a group of primary school children of mixed ages, in which the majority have never been trained in a Montessori class or in no proper school at all, so that none of them has been normalized.

It is often assumed that normalization through the Montessori method is expected to take place at the ages of 3 or 4. A few older children may be admitted, too, and although in their case the beneficial results of Montessori upbringing may neither be quick enough nor deep enough to be satisfactory, they can get some benefit without the class becoming adversely affected by their slow progress. But what if the majority, or all of the children in a primary class are neither normalized nor properly trained for independent work, unable to concentrate, unwilling to learn, and not at all anxious to discipline themselves?

The conventional way in such cases is for the teacher to be hard and strict from the start — punishing severely the smallest transgressions and, for better control of the individuals, doing mainly collective exercises after a short lesson, all students doing the same work, so that an eye can be kept on every child, to prevent any unauthorized word or gesture.

After a few days of such a regime of terror, the teacher relaxes a little, allowing certain liberties, but pounces at the children again if any sign of disorder appears. The advocates of this way of education may assume that once a child has learned to obey, it will not only learn its lessons, but it will do anything else that is expected of it, and thus will become normalized by acquiring good habits of behavior. Such an assumption does not, however, seem to be confirmed by the facts, and it cannot be justified by either logic or psychology. And it is certainly contrary to Montessori principles of education. The question, therefore, is whether it is at all possible to normalize a whole class of primary school children without resorting to the dictatorial measures and "carrot-and-stick" procedures used in conventional teaching.

Speaking from personal experience gained in several schools where I was faced with situations such as those just described, I am convinced that the answer to this question is a categorical: yes.

For the benefit of teachers who may have to deal with similar situations, let me describe certain procedures and methods that I have found effective.

First a word of caution. It is the mental attitude of the teacher that is all-important here. If the teacher believes that children can be educated by being treated like caged beasts who do not like to be taught, and if left by themselves would always prefer to play rather than do school work, he cannot hope to make much progress in achieving self-discipline. The teacher must first persuade himself, even against apparently contrary evidence, that all children can and will learn with pleasure, even enthusiastically, if the conditions of work are right.

Now a practical remark: Whatever teachers do, they must remember that they have a real-life situation to handle, not a laboratory specimen where all the conditions are under their control. When teaching in a school, teachers must at the same time satisfy the children, their parents, and the school authorities — and pretty quickly too. So compromises must be made.

First, a compromise with the children: The teacher must gain the children's respect, love, and confidence, both collectively and individually. He should try to find out as much as possible about the previous year's teaching, materials, and textbooks used, as well as about the ages and standards of the children in the class. The classroom should be inspected and the condition of the environment, including all teaching aids, checked. If there are any books or materials needed, they should be ordered at once. A sufficient amount should be ordered, to ensure having the right material at all the necessary levels. As for the number of copies to be ordered, it is better to err on the generous side, for some enthusiastic children often surpass all expectations in the rate of progress, while others fall below their apparent ability.

On the first day, the teacher should call the children to a meeting and have them talk about their previous teacher, their holidays, or anything about which they may like to talk. It helpful to find out a lot about each child, assess their intelligence and see who are likely to become leaders, because these are the children the teacher must have on his side in case of a conflict. Then the teacher should explain the way in which he expects them to work. Radical changes should not be made, but the children should grasp that things are going to be somewhat different from before, not because the teacher wants it to be so, but for their own good, to allow them to learn better and have more pleasure in doing so. The children should be shown where various materials or books are going to be kept, and at this first session the teacher should find out at least whether they all know how to use them.

The teacher should show himself to be confident, efficient and friendly, not standing any nonsense, but not lacking a sense of humor. The children should be told a few rules of behavior expected during lessons, at playtime, and at lunch. They should not be told too many rules to start with, but it should be ensured they all listen and understand what the teacher means. At one of the first meetings the teacher should discuss various duties to be undertaken by individuals regarding the maintenance of order on the shelves, the feeding of animals or watering of plants, keeping the weather chart, and so on.

The second compromise must be made regarding the parents. They will all ask their children if they like the school and if the teacher was nice. Soon they will be asking them what they have done in school on a particular day and if they have learned something. So children cannot be allowed to wander about or play games all day long. There must be something they can be allowed to do that they can quote as a "learning occupation." In order to do this, the teacher has to find out in the shortest possible time the standard of work each is capable of in reading, writing, spelling, and arithmetic, so that they can each be given the right kind of book or assignment, without having to spend time in lengthy explanations.

Finally, teachers must compromise with their superiors. Superiors will not bother them much in the first few weeks as long as there are no problems with the children and no complaints are received from the parents. But they will certainly expect the teacher to have a reasonably quiet atmosphere in the classroom, keeping all children busy with something. If the class is unruly at the beginning, they should be taken out a lot or allowed to sit around in a circle to talk with the teacher. The teacher can also play a quiet record or read them a story — anything that will keep them reasonably peaceful.

The most difficult thing to obtain when starting a free class of the Montessori type is the elimination of noise. As said before, this can only be achieved gradually, by individuals getting thoroughly absorbed in their work, which is a distant objective for a collection of children who start off by being completely untrained — or who have been "trained" the wrong way. But even at the beginning, the teacher must always be able to obtain silence when he wants to talk to the children, when he expects a visitor to the class, or at any time when the noise becomes oppressive.

There are various methods for obtaining momentary silence, and every teacher must discover the way that best suits him. Some teachers ring a bell and expect everyone to "freeze" and listen to whatever they have to say. Others announce: "5 minutes of silence, please" and get the desired effect, if only for a short while. I knew a teacher of a very undisciplined class, who never raised her voice and used an amazingly simple, yet effective means of obtaining silence when the children were sitting in a circle and one or two of them would constantly talk or laugh and not bother to listen. Instead of saying: "Jimmy, be quiet now," "Joseph, why are you talking?" "Denise, put that book away," and so on, she would look around and pick out children who were sitting quietly, saying in a quiet voice: "Christy is sitting very quietly, Mark is very quiet, too," and so on. These words seemed to have a magical effect on the others who did not want to be outdone by Christy, Mark, or anyone else. In a few minutes, everyone in the circle was quiet and ready to listen.

I have tried to apply a similar method before lunchtime in order to obtain an orderly start to the meal. I would make all the children sit in a circle, and I would choose one boy or girl to decide who was the quietest and to give that child a sign to get up. The child pointed out was then expected to go very quietly to fetch its lunch box and start eating. Then another child would be indicated, and so on. This worked almost as well as the previously described method, with the added advantage that I was not involved in deciding who was and who was not quiet. As there were many candidates for doing the "picking," we later decided that the pickers should take turns in alphabetical order, a different one every day, and that no one should be missed. The children liked the idea, collaborated with it well, and received an additional incentive for learning the alphabet if they had previously had difficulty memorizing the order of letters.

So far we have been talking of expedience, of compromises during the transitional period before the normalization process has started to work in earnest. Now we come to the main plan of action. I have found that the greatest obstacle to proper behavior and learning application is not the unwillingness of children to make the effort, but either a fear of boredom or a fear of failure. Owing to its previous experiences maybe, a child would shun work, being convinced that learning must be a very distasteful business (otherwise surely the teacher would not be so anxious to make him do it). However, what is most difficult for children who have never before worked in a Montessori school, is first to decide what work to do; then to concentrate on working with it for some time; and finally, to do it without oral instructions or help from the teacher or anyone else. Even when a teacher helps a child by telling it what it is supposed to do, the child will want the teacher to stand over it and direct every movement, every word or figure, so that it can be sure the teacher approves.

Concentration is perhaps the most important quality that children develop through early Montessori education. If they have not developed concentration before the age of 5, it usually takes a long time and much effort to acquire it later. Out of concentration grows confidence, and after that comes initiative, creativeness, and, the crown of the entire normalizing process, love of and devotion to work. The first thing, therefore, that teachers should direct their efforts to, is getting children to concentrate individually on any sort of useful occupation, whether playing with bricks, painting, modeling, making airplanes out of paper, or playing checkers.

Before being able to concentrate on an individual occupation, children will want to work or play in groups of two, three, or four, watching others at work and trying to join them. This invariably causes a lot of discussion and argument, hence a lot of noise — but it is a noise with a creative potential, like the sound of a car engine starting on a cold day, before it has warmed up. Although some children at that stage will construct very attractive toys with building blocks, others may well prefer to play with them afterward and instead indulge in make-believe games with their classmates during lesson time. But even that is better than running around the classroom disturbing the others, scattering materials about, or destroying whatever object they can find.

People who are not acquainted with this kind of educational procedure, even teachers, find this type of activity a sheer waste of time — spoiling the children and failing to teach them anything of academic value. It is therefore important to stress to the parents concerned that the nonacademic stage of this education is only temporary. The school's authorities should also be in agreement on this matter. In any case, not all the children will have to start their re-education from the very beginning, and some may be ready and willing to do their "three Rs" assignments immediately.

Whatever they do in these initial stages, teachers cannot expect everything to go smoothly. There will be breaches of discipline; children shouting and fighting, damaging the equipment or losing valuable pieces, or refusing to put back the books and materials used; and so on. The teacher must not panic, nor shout at transgressors, lose his temper or despair of ever having success with the group. He should be prepared to be teased, provoked, insulted, and cursed. But he should keep talking to the children every morning in a circle, get their approval for introducing new rules for keeping order as necessity demands, and point out the fact that at school they have to learn and not waste their time. Every child should be given clear instructions for doing assignments appropriate to its capacities, reading, tracing, working out sums with the help of some materials, and so on, so that each one can do it all without extra help, directly after the meeting. A list of the children can be made and put up on the wall, with the teacher placing a mark at each name as they accomplish their assignments for the day. At first the assignment work should be limited to as little as 30 to 40 minutes. Gradually the work to be done can be increased, but care should be taken to ensure it is the right sort — not too hard, or there will be too many children needing the teacher's help, but not too easy either, or they will get bored.

Applying too much pressure will meet with resistance, and the educational work, which should be aimed at voluntary self-discipline, will be retarded. Diplomacy is necessary. Some favorite structural materials such as blocks could be kept in limited supply so that no more than a few children at a time can use them. It may then be suggested to the children that those who finish their assignments first should have priority in using the most popular materials.

After a few weeks there will probably be an increasing number of children who find pleasure in their academic work, some may even ask for more and may want to continue working at home, particularly over weekends. On the other hand, if a child is slow in its work, the teacher can suggest that work be finished during break time — while the classroom aide takes the others outside to the playground. This should not be done as a punishment, but as a way of giving the child undivided attention and help. Most children accept this plan willingly, and others will sometimes ask to be allowed to join them. Yet there will still be days when everything goes wrong, for some unknown reason, but the good working days will be more frequent, and the working periods will become longer.

I discovered one way of awakening dormant enthusiasm in a creatively rather unresponsive group, by encouraging them to write their own little stories or poems. I had the children write down their ideas in any way they liked, without bothering about correct lettering or spelling. I then typed their literary creations without amending anything except the spelling and punctuation. The next day, they were invited to read them to the class during a circle meeting. Those who could not write could dictate their stories to me. Most of them could not read them loud enough or with proper diction, so I had to read them again for the group to hear. I found this way not only helped improve the children's grammar and spelling, but it made them learn to put their ideas and feelings into words. Moreover, I often got a revealing insight into their unconscious desires, longings, or fears through the choice of their subjects and the manner of expressing them.

Following are some examples of children's spontaneous compositions, classified by age:

THE FARMER
Once upon a time there lived a farmer on a farm.
He had cows, ducks, sheep and chicks,
and he had so many children. He was so rich,
he had money.
THE END (by Nicole D., 6 years old)

THE CAT THAT COULD WHISTLE
There lived a cat named Peanuts,
And all his brothers and sisters laughed at him.
He went to his mother's office.
They went on a trip to New Mexico.
While he was on the plane,
He whistled for a little while.
(by Mitchell McG., 6 years 2 months)

THE DONKEY
Once upon a time there was a donkey. He was very fat
because he ate mushrooms. One day he was eating
mushrooms, and then suddenly BOOOOM! he turned into a
mushroom. He put on his roller skates and then skated all
over to Mr. Mushroom. And then the donkey said: "Can you
change me back into a donkey?" "Of course I can" and then
he laughed. "Here, eat this mushroom, and then you'll turn
back into a donkey". So he ate the mushroom, and he was a
donkey once more.
THE END (by Peter M., 6 years 6 months)

A POEM CALLED "HI"
When I go to school
I say "Hi" to my friends.
It is a nice word.
When I say it I get really good.
THE END. (by Peter M., 6 years 6 months)

APPLES
An apple is red.
Red apples are good.

I like them.
Apples.
(by Sakinah M., 7 years 2 months)

SCHOOL
My school, it is fun.
I like school.
I like my friends.
In school. (by Sakinah M., 7 years 2 months)

THE BLACK GIRL
I am black like a black cat.
A black cat is me.
I am black and beautiful.
The black queen of me.
(by Sakinah M., 7 years 2 months)

ME
I am me.
I like me.
I like me a lot.
(by Sakinah M., 7 years 2 months)

THE BIRD THAT COULDN'T SING
There lived a bird who could not sing,
So he asked the rabbit to help.
The rabbit said: "Go see the wise old owl,
He knows everything".
So the bird went to the owl,
And the owl told him that he was to open his mouth.
(by Daniel C., 7 years 5 months)

There is always more likelihood of unruliness on rainy days, when the children cannot use their surplus energy in the playground. On such occasions it is useful to give them a lesson of "physical jerks" or "movements" as some children call it. I believe that every teacher should have a repertoire of exercises that he can practice together with the children. Here is a set of "daily 15" that I like to do myself every day:

1. Stand straight, legs apart, arms raised upward. Take a deep breath, then bend down a few times (touching your toes if you can). Repeat six times.

2. Stand as in Exercise 1, arms pointing right and left. Twist your trunk left and right (with arms outstretched) six times.

3. Standing in the same position as in Exercise 2, let the arms describe circles in the air, small and large. Six circles in forward direction, six in reverse.

4. Lie down on the floor with face down, legs apart, arms stretched out in front. Do swimming movements with the arms as in breaststroke, joining the legs every time the arms complete a circle. Six movements.

5. Push-ups. Lie on the floor as in Exercise 4. Put your hands under your chest, the palms touching the floor. Keep your whole body rigid and straighten your arms, raising yourself above the floor. Repeat six times slowly.

6. Lying, face down, as in Exercise 4, get hold of your ankles, then by pressing with your feet backward raise the upper part of your body. Six times slowly.

7. Turn on your back, with hands folded behind your neck. Lift your legs alternately, without bending, six times.

8. Keeping the same position, describe small circles in the air with both legs. Six times outward and six times the reverse.

9. Still lying on your back, bend your knees and grip them with both hands trying to make them touch your chin. Six times.

10. Now lift your legs and the lower pan of your back, so that the feet point upward and the back is supported by your hands, the elbows resting on the floor. Then do cycling movements with your legs in the air 12 times.

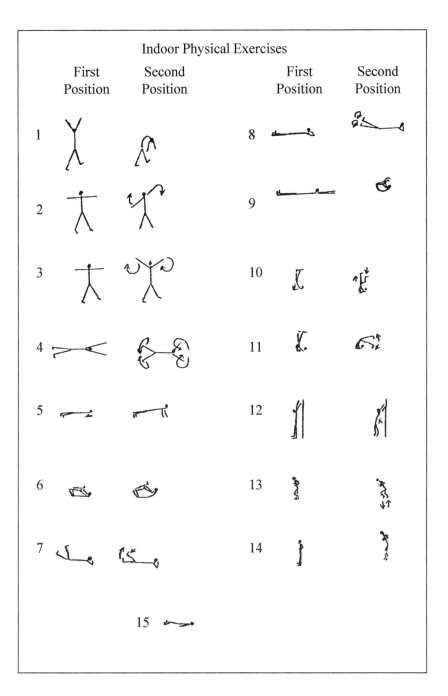

Indoor Physical Exercises

	First Position	Second Position			First Position	Second Position

Sketches by the author for indoor physical exercises.

11. Still keeping the position as in Exercise 10, swing your legs backward, alternately touching the floor behind your head with your toes. Six times with each leg.

12. Stand up against the wall at one foot (the child's foot) distance. Lift up your arms and bend backward so as to touch the wall with your fingers. Now stand up on your toes, expanding your chest and breathe in slowly. Twelve times. A very useful exercise. If there is not enough wall space available for all children, they can stand wherever they are and bend backward during breathing, as far as they can.

13. Stand in a circle and move your legs as if you were running, but don't move from your place. Do it first slowly, then quicker and quicker, for a full minute.

14. Without changing position, start jumping up with your feet only, higher and higher for 1 minute, putting in the greatest effort possible.

15. Lie down on the floor and relax. Breathe normally. Imagine that a heavy blanket is pressing you down, making any movement of your limbs impossible. Stay like this until you are completely relaxed, thinking of something quiet and pleasant or of nothing at all. Finally, get up and sit down to some quiet work.

Despite all the teacher's efforts, there may still be some children who refuse to work and obey rules, defying his authority and stretching his patience to the limit. Talking over these problems with the child's parents may be of some help, but often the teacher will find that the parents, or the single parent in charge, have very little control over the child's behavior themselves or use drastic measures that the teacher would not approve. In that case, a personal, individual approach to the child will need to be developed, to try to find out how matters can be helped. One approach is to make a "contract" with the child — to ask it to help keep order in the classroom, and if it agrees, the child should be reminded of its promise first thing in the morning, in private. Another way is to consult with other teachers who know the child, or to ask the advice of a psychologist. But more often than not the best help will come from the class itself. As the general working atmosphere in the class improves, the obstreperous individuals will be drawn into it, and become more cooperative.

This brings us back to the importance of meetings. Apart from dealing with the daily business and work problems, there should be opportunity for leading the children's attention to broader issues, to social and moral problems such as the need for fairness, and for gratitude for good things received. Children can be asked to name persons or animals to whom we should be grateful: the cows that give us milk, the bees that collect the honey, the farmers who grow our food, the bakers who bake our bread and cakes, the tailors who make our clothes, the builders who make our houses, the parents who take care of the children and work hard to earn money for all the expenses, and so on. Reaching out further, the gratitude can be extended to the sun and the wind, the rain and the flowers, the beauty of nature and finally God, the Maker of the universe[55].

Talks like that help turn children's minds to issues outside their narrow circle of interest, and indirectly ease the discipline problem by bringing the teacher and children closer together and helping them understand each other.

5

Teacher and Children

This chapter begins by quoting from Montessori's article on the "Spiritual Preparation of the Teacher," published in the <u>Rivista Montessori</u> of September/October 1932. Here it is, in my translation from the Italian:

> A teacher would be deceiving himself if he thought that he could be well prepared for his mission only by acquiring certain knowledge. Because he must, above anything else, create within himself certain qualities of moral character. ... We must stress the need for the teacher to prepare himself internally, examining himself thoroughly in order to rid his soul of any defects which might become a hindrance in dealing with a child. ... To be educators, we do not have to become "perfect," devoid of any weakness. A person constantly preoccupied with perfecting themselves inwardly may remain unaware of those defects which prevent them from understanding the child. So we have to learn and to allow ourselves to be "guided." We have to be educated if we want to educate. ...

> Now this is our concrete help: "<u>The deadly sin which rises inside us and prevents us from understanding the child is Anger</u>".

> And because no sin appears alone, without the company of another, Anger becomes associated with a different sin, of noble appearance, but even more devilish: Pride. Anger ... — becoming fused with pride, generates that set of actions of innocent and respectable appearance that is called <u>tyranny</u>. ... The preparation that our method requires from the teacher consists of an inward search, to find if he is free from the deadly sins of tyranny. He has to root out from his heart the old crust of anger and pride. To become humble. Henceforth to become clothed with charity. These are the inner qualities he must

become endowed with. . . . We are not saying that he has to approve all the child's doings, or refrain from expressing his opinion, or do nothing to enhance the development of the child's mind or emotions. On the contrary, he must not forget that his task is to "educate", to be the child's real teacher. But an act of humility must come first, the eradication of a prejudice that has taken root in our hearts. . . . We do not want to abolish the help which education holds out to the child; but only that inward state of mind, that attitude of adults which prevents them from understanding him.

Let us see now what positive directions Montessori recommended to the teacher. Here are 10 points listed under the heading of "A Decalogue," in the magazine <u>Around the Child</u>[56].

1. Never touch a child unless invited by him (in some way or other).

2. Never speak ill of the child in his presence or absence.

3. Concentrate on strengthening and helping the development of what is good in the child, so that its presence may leave less and less space for evil.

4. Be proactive in preparing the environment, take meticulous and constant care of it. Help the child establish constructive relations with it. Show the proper place where the means of development are kept and demonstrate their proper use.

5. Be ever ready to answer the call of the child who stands in need of you, and always listen and respond to the child who appeals to you.

6. Respect the child who makes a mistake and can then or later correct it himself, but stop firmly and immediately any misuse of the environment and any action which endangers the child, its own development or that of others.

7. Respect the child who takes a rest or watches others working or ponders over what he himself has done or will do. Neither call him nor force him to other forms of activity.

8. Help those who are in search of activity and cannot find it.

9. Be untiring in repeating presentations to the child who refused them earlier, in helping the child to acquire what is not yet his own and to overcome imperfections. Do this by animating the environment, with care, with purposive restraint and silence, with mild words and loving presence. Make your ready presence felt to the child who searches, and hide from the child who has found.

10. Always treat the child with the best of good manners and offer him the best you have in yourself and at your disposal.

Many teachers will find these words a bit too poetic and sentimental. It must be remembered that when Montessori spoke of the child, she usually had in mind the little defenseless 3- or 4-year-old. Point 1 means that the teacher should not caress or cuddle a child unless the child asks for it, and even then with discretion, because other children may become jealous. A teacher would have to be a saint to keep rigorously to Point 2. Point 3 is quite right, although rather vague and prone to multiple interpretations. Point 4 is rather important. The success of the whole method ultimately depends on preparing a proper environment and its constant improvement and care. Point 5 seems somewhat idealistic if taken too literally. Just think of a teacher who has three or four calls for help from different children at the same time either because their workbooks are not ideally clear, or because the children have not had enough practice in following written instructions, or simply because they want the teacher's attention. Points 6 through 9 depend very much on the tact and discretion of the teacher, and are much easier to apply to small children than to those of elementary school age (e.g. how are we to know whether a child who writes a clumsy figure 5, starting from the bottom, will not get into a wrong habit that will be harder to get rid of as he gets older?). Some children always expect the teacher to find them an occupation. They need to be encouraged to use their own will and imagination and decide what to do by themselves. Finally, with regard to presentations of materials, at the elementary school level they are often complicated and lengthy, and repeating them frequently may take too much of the teacher's time. It is therefore necessary to rely on the presentation offered by the written or printed instructions, which the child may be asked to study again.

Allowing for certain adjustments and change of wording here and there, however, taken as a whole, the "decalogue" expresses well the attitude to be taken toward children, irrespective of age, gender, and temperament.

An interesting illustration of the teacher's responsibilities in a Montessori class was given by Hélène Lubienska de Lenval[57] (who was my first wife). She compared the effect of the teacher's work in the class to the algebraic multiplication of positive and negative numbers. As we know, in algebra the four rules are that:

$$(+a) \times (+b) = + ab$$
$$(-a) \times (+b) = - ab$$
$$(+a) \times (-b) = - ab$$
$$(-a) \times (-b) = + ab$$

with the puzzling (and for some people difficult to understand) result that "minus times minus gives plus."

She made the following use of the algebraic symbols:

"a" means teacher
"b" means child
"+" means helps, child's useful efforts, development
" -" means hinders, child's useless efforts, deviation
"=" means result
"x" means the general influence of the teacher on the child.

Four different life situations are the outcome of this application of algebraic rules: If the teacher's (a) action (x):
    helps (+) the useful (+) efforts of the child (b),
        the result (=) is development (+)
    helps (+) the useless (-) efforts of the child (b),
        the result (-) is deviation (-)
    hinders (-) the useful (+) efforts of the child (b),
        the result (=) is deviation (-)
    hinders (-) the useless (-) efforts of the child (b),
        the result (=) is development (+)

The quality of the teacher can be estimated by his general attitude toward children. His task can be compared to that of a salesman. Imagine a salesman approaching his clients with a deeply rooted idea that he is doing his work merely for a living, and that the clients could well do without his services, but that he must somehow persuade them to buy his merchandise, otherwise he will lose his job. Such a salesperson would never be a success. However, a salesperson who is convinced and can transmit that conviction to the clients, — that they are being offered a marvelous device, and that they are lucky to have someone bring it to their knowledge, thus making their work lighter, giving them more pleasure in life, and increasing their earning capacity in future — will surely be a greater success in making a sale.

A teacher has to be like a salesman. He is selling knowledge and skill to his clients, the children. If he believes that the children would actually prefer to stay at home or play outside than do the lessons, and that without the threat of punishment he will never be able to keep order, he can only hope for minimum effort from his pupils and mediocre results. If, however, on the contrary he believes in the positive qualities and the will to learn inherent in every child, and that his task is merely to discover what interests the child and how to satisfy him, there will be few children who fail to respond.

It is said that there are no bad soldiers, only bad generals. In the same way, it can be said that there are no bad pupils, only bad teachers. What every teacher needs is experience. He must find out ways that work. And he must be ready to change his methods if the desired goal, namely an increase in spontaneous work and the development of a positive, creative personality — in short, normalization — does not appear as a result. This is the whole essence of Montessori.

In the following pages I outline some practical hints and suggestions that seem to promote that goal, although I realize that the subject will by no means be exhausted, and that other teachers may be able to add more useful devices, or may disagree with some of the practices proposed in this book.

Order in the classroom is something organic that has to grow and cannot be expected right from the beginning. The teacher must not panic because of occasional chaos, and should not try to oppose it by drastic measures, causing a precedent he will be forced to follow in other similar situations. He should rather try to give everyone something interesting to do — or occupy them all with some collective activity.

Here are some general "Dos" and "Don'ts" to remember:

1. **DO**: Pay attention to the environment, both within and outside the classroom. See that it is sufficiently equipped, according to the number and ages of children in the class. You should be constantly trying to improve it, make it more attractive and neat, and encourage the children to keep it in good condition. Keep some living things in the classroom — plants, flowers, and small animals, and show the children how to look after them. Make it easy for children to keep things in order by giving clear instructions and adequate space for everything, providing pegs or lockers for outer garments, individual shelves for each child's books and school-work, extra space for larger creations, and so on.

2. **DO**: Watch your attitude to children. Keep your voice low, avoid having noisy activities in the classroom, show a friendly and smiling face, and take it for granted that no matter what the children do or miss doing, they intrinsically always want to be good, and that they have a feeling of failure if they don't do the right thing. The most important thing, therefore, is to strengthen their self-confidence and feeling of security, without which there can be no real progress.

3. **DO**: Keep an eye on children. Like the conductor of an orchestra, you should know at all times what each child is doing, and how it is doing it. Children should feel free to choose their work, but watch out for an opportunity to direct their attention to other occupations in which their progress may have been neglected. Try to find ways to fire their imagination and inspire them to work. Give them small responsibilities, such as watering plants; feeding the animals and cleaning their cages; keeping a temperature chart, weather chart, or attendance record daily. Read them stories about history and geography; have them write or dictate to someone short stories, letters, or poems; awaken their civic consciousness by telling them about daily events, festivals, and anniversaries, provoking their questions. Discuss

examples of courtesy, generosity, and fair play — or the opposite. In short, build up their minds and broaden their outlook by making them think of things other than themselves; and after every little talk or lecture give suggestions for some drawing, writing, or other work in which they could express their impressions or feelings. Keep a regular record of all children's progress.

4. **DO**: Watch out for lonely, silent, unhappy children. Bring them back into the group. Don't allow cruel teasing or bullying. Help those who find it difficult to decide what to do with appropriate suggestions, and give moral support to voluntary enterprises for organizing amateur plays, puppet shows, contests, and so on. Do what you can to make the class an organic unity, a social group conscious of its aims, with its members acting together. Respect its leaders and try to have them on your side in any difficult situation. It will help you have influence on the whole group.

5. **DO**: Be creative and help the children to be so. Unless you are constantly finding new ways of teaching and organizing your activities, instead of following some ready pattern of instructions or orders from your superiors, you will not get satisfaction from your work, and the quality of your teaching and educating will suffer. In the same way, support every good creative effort of the children themselves, their way of learning, playing, organizing, and finding a solution to daily problems. Share their games and you will learn a great deal from them. You will also find yourself closer to the whole group and more able to lead them.

6. **DON'T**: Leave the classroom in a condition you would not like the children to find on entering. Never leave materials lying about that have been damaged, have a piece missing, or are otherwise unusable. Don't keep in evidence odd tins or bowls with broken crayons, screws, buttons, or other items having no fixed abode. Don't let children's drawings or other work lie untidily or occupy valuable space unnecessarily.

7. **DON'T**: Be too familiar with children, kissing them and petting for your own pleasure instead of waiting until they show they need it. Be careful not to show preference for a particular child in a way that may provoke the jealousy of other children; fight your aversion to those who

are less cooperative, so they do not feel that you don't care for them as much as for the others.

8. **DON'T**: Ever despair of normalizing a child who resists all your efforts to get it seriously interested in some work. Sylvia Ashton-Warner said, "So long as the mind of the infant is still malleable, it is not too late"[58], and this applies also to older children, and surprisingly, to adults too. Signs of recovery sometimes come suddenly, when least expected. Don't think that an occupation that you would find boring and tedious is also distasteful to children. I remember once in the classroom soapy water was accidentally spilled on the floor, and I was wondering whom I would ask to clean up the mess. Then suddenly a 6-year-old girl asked permission to mop it up. I consented of course, and she did the job beautifully, with obvious satisfaction. Another time, I spoke rather acidly to a boy who had the habit of scribbling all over his desk, saying that it was time he should scrub it clean. To my astonishment, the boy did not resent my remark, but cleaned the desk most earnestly, and with visible pleasure. Other children followed his example without further prompting, and soon all desks had a new sparkling appearance.

9. **DON'T**: Take yourself too seriously. Have a sense of humor and humanity. Don't require instant obedience, just "because you say so." Children sometimes have a rude way of telling off the teacher for interfering or being lazy or uncooperative. A child once gave me a lesson when I spoke to her rather sharply during class-sweeping time. She said indignantly: "Why don't YOU pick it up?". I didn't know what to answer, not that she was right — a teacher should never do the work when it is the children's turn to do it, otherwise he could not supervise them — but it was the child's way of saying that I was rude. I should have apologized. I didn't. But that remark made me feel like a fool and I never forgot it. So, if the children are right and you are wrong, don't be too proud to admit your error; they will love you for it and will become more willing to listen to your words in future. To prevent losing face, avoid asking a child to do something if you expect the answer will be No! Don't tell the child "this is easy" if he may subsequently find it too difficult, causing him to become depressed and discouraged by failure, and don't tell him "you will find it too difficult" when he is eager to attempt something. It is better to say: "I will show

it to you another time" or "You should practice doing . . . first."
Before speaking to a group, wait until they stop talking, but once there
is silence, don't hesitate, trying to find the right words, be ready to
speak at once, slowly and clearly, or you will lose the best moment for
their attention.

10.**DON'T**: Speak to the child in a way you would not speak to a guest in
your home, don't humiliate him, hurt him by insulting or sarcastic
words, don't administer physical or moral pain as a deterrent or
repressive measure. C.S. Lewis, who cannot be accused of having an
anti-adult bias, wrote:

> We heard a great deal about the rudeness of the rising
> generation. I am an oldster myself and might be expected to
> take the oldsters' side, but in fact I have been far more impressed
> by the bad manners of parents to children than by those of
> children to parents. . . . Dogmatic assertions on matters which
> the children understand and the elders don't, ruthless
> interruptions, flat contradictions, ridicule of things the young
> take seriously — sometimes their religion — insulting
> references to their friends, all provide an easy answer to the
> question "Why are they always out? Why do they like every
> house better than their home?". Who does not prefer civility to
> barbarism?[59]

Substitute "teachers" for "parents" and "school" for "home," and the same
remarks will apply to some of the teachers.

Regarding the mental abuse of children, a more subtle way of humiliating
children is refusing to treat them as mature and responsible humans to the
extent to which they can be trusted to be. This applies particularly to the
system of giving marks or awards for their work or good behavior. One
reason given for awarding marks or placing children in a list according to
performance is to stimulate competition. In fact, it brings results only
with a few children at the top of the list. It makes little difference to the
others whether they are, say, number 9 or 13, whereas for the last few on
the list the awareness of being so far from the top is rather depressing.
The mere fact of giving awards and evaluations is in itself wrong because
it gives the children the wrong motivation, and makes them feel that in the
opinion of the teachers they would never do the schoolwork without

incentives. The result is that in the eyes of the children, working for the pure love of study appears to be sheer lunacy.

The main objection to marks, however, is that they register only the achievement, which is largely the result of being born with a good memory and potential intelligence. But what really matters is not the amount of knowledge acquired but the effort children put in, and the extent to which they manage to assimilate their knowledge and fuse it with what they already know — but this sort of thing can never be properly assessed and quantitatively measured.

For the comfort of teachers who worry about their pupils' progress, I add: Don't expect 100% success from any single child or group. No system has been invented that has no failures at all. The best we can do is to give the children a fair chance of reaching the expected standard, with as much encouragement and guidance as we are capable of, without exerting ourselves beyond reasonable limits. No one can force a child to learn if it is not willing to cooperate. If it learns under pressure, it will not remember the things learned for very long.

The best way of getting children's cooperation is to discuss most problems at a class meeting "dealing with each situation as a communal problem", as H.R. Kohl suggested[60]. Meetings should be held at regular intervals or whenever either the teacher or some children wish to raise a matter of common interest, such as the rearrangement of work schedules, distribution of daily duties, dealing with antisocial behavior of a member of the class, disposition of furniture and materials, organization of a show or excursion, and so on. A meeting should not last long, but plenty of time should be given to children to express their opinions. A vote should decide on the acceptance or rejection of a proposal. The children should feel that the way they vote will decide the action they will be expected to take or the responsibility they will assume. In other words, they have to realize that they are bound by the decision they take. In some important issues, the teacher or a member of the governing body will have to give approval to a decision. But on the whole, it is not likely that children would wish to pass a resolution conflicting with the school regulations or interfere with the teacher's responsibilities. Children not attending a meeting should not be excused from conforming to the decisions taken in their absence.

It takes a great deal of tact and skill for the teacher to make class meetings effective and to influence them discreetly without appearing to do so. But the results can be immensely rewarding. In the first place, meetings teach the children to think, to speak in public, and to make their opinions prevail against those of their opponents. They also make them listen to other people's points of view and to consider their interests. They teach them the proper use of freedom and prepare for their future responsibilities as citizens in a democratic state. As Kohl said, "the democratic development of routines and rules and restrictions is . . . crucial to the development of freedom"[61].

However, deciding by majority vote is not always a solution to a problem. There may be a minority of dissatisfied children who feel their case did not have proper consideration.   This is a flaw in many apparently democratic institutions that make a fetish of the rights of the majority, with disregard for the needs and the feelings of the dissenting minority of individuals.   The minority may be right after all (intelligent people are often a minority). The majority decision may be stupid, vulgar, or morally wrong. The minority may become unjustly oppressed, thwarted in their desire to expand, to create, to live a fuller and more worthwhile existence; such a situation often occurs in political or religious organizations.

Respect for a minority is one of the basic principles of the Montessori system, which started by calling for consideration of the rights of a minority, namely the children.   So children too should learn how to tolerate dissenting voices in their midst, make a compromise with them or allow the minority group to make its own, different arrangements, as long as it does not clash with the interests of the others. Teaching children how to solve their problems while paying regard to other people's interests and feelings is one of the foremost tasks of school education, possibly more important than teaching geography or mathematics! A true Montessori classroom should be not only a center of academic learning, it should also become a training ground for the responsibilities of future adults, whether they be manual workers or intellectuals, business men or trade union members, leaders of voluntary organizations or politicians, a kind of embryonic little society.

But education for democracy is by no means the only educational benefit of working through, and in, meetings. Meetings teach children not to be merely carrying out duties imposed on them by the school program, but to take the initiative in collective enterprises of any kind, to organize themselves for some positive task, with faith and self-confidence, and to be ready to do great things never attempted before.

In a class of 6- to 9-year-olds I once taught, a few children told me they wanted to give a puppet show. We arranged the room accordingly, set up chairs for the nonplayers as audience, and waited. What was meant to be a show was just a few improvised sentences read aloud by one girl, while some puppets representing a man and a tiger were hitting each other mercilessly, making the young audience laugh. The "show" continued until everyone became bored. Still, it was a first attempt, so I said a few encouraging words, added a few suggestions for future improvement, and left it at that.

As Christmas drew near, one of the girls decided to write a play similar to one that she had seen on TV, with Mary and Jesus and various animals taking part. She got other children to help, and together they decided to have the whole class participate. It was an ambitious plan, involving rehearsals and the cooperation of all the children. I tried to offer some advice, but was told to mind my own business. They wanted to do it their way. Then there were difficulties concerning who was to get the more dignified roles, such as those of Mary and Joseph and the angels, and who was to be a pig or a donkey. Some players got upset and wanted to back out, risking the collapse of the whole show. I had to call them together and let them air their grievances, until all was well again. The parents helped with the costumes, and my aide played on her guitar the music to accompany the carol singers. We invited the children of the younger class and as many parents as were able to come, and the play was a great success.

A few months went by, until one day, the children said they had arranged a play about Snow White and the Seven Dwarfs which would be held in the classroom the next day. They had written the words and distributed the roles, done the rehearsals, fixed the day for the play, and sent invitations to parents, all by themselves. The performance went without a hitch. I did not have a say in it, did not help them at all, and yet, indirectly, I thought of it as my greatest achievement in the whole school year.

More detailed suggestions about teaching are discussed here. Following is a general timetable that I found useful with 6- to 9-year-olds:

Morning:

8:30 to 9:00	Children arrive at school, and are greeted.
9:00 to 10:00	Work takes place on the most important subject for each child, using workbooks or materials with the help of coaching.
10:00 to 10:15	Break, fruit juice, and snack.
10:15 to 11:15	Change of subject, individual coaching continued.
11:15 to 11:30	Children report the work completed to the teacher.
11:30 to 12:00	Playground activities.
12:00 to 1:00	Lunch, followed by quiet reading.

Afternoon:

1:00 to 2:30	Afternoon occupations — according to the day of the week: carrying out larger projects, art, craftwork, dancing lessons, music, singing, going to the library, excursions (field trips), pursuing any individual interests, care of plants or pets kept in the classroom, educational games.
2:30 to 3:00	Playground (but children on duty for sweeping the classroom stay in at first).
3:00	Parents pick up the children. End of school day.

Children should start their most important work as soon as they come to school, changing their timetable only when necessary. Otherwise, there should be room for considerable freedom for children to organize their study according to their preferences. Some children may not wish to take the morning break but may want to continue working until the time for going to the playground or lunch. Sometimes good weather makes everyone want to stay out longer. But failing any special reason it is advisable to maintain a program. Children over age 9 who can work longer without a break may eat lunch later, too. They also require more diversification of their work. Hence, the class may have to be split into several groups, each having a different timetable. Generally speaking, it is not good to have too much of an age difference in one classroom, unless there are many specialized teachers and different subject rooms, each supplied with appropriate materials and reference books, as well as areas reserved for quiet work and others where noisy exercises can be carried out without disturbing those who need to concentrate. Children between 5 and 7 have a different rhythm and pace of work than do 8- and 9-year-olds. The younger children do better work when they are in a separate classroom with a different teacher. Children ages 10 and older would benefit from having a number of specialist teachers, each responsible for keeping the materials and books of his own specialty. The material and knowledge required for individualized study has now become so vast and complicated that no single teacher can be sufficiently acquainted with all of it to make a proper selection for purchase, not to speak of having the ability to help children at a moment's notice, say, skipping from a grammar difficulty to an algebra problem and then again to handling a chemical experiment. The divisions into age groups should take into account individual children's ability and temperament, rather than dividing them by age only.

With the youngest group, each child should be met at the door with a personal greeting. They should look the teacher straight in the face with a hearty handshake and a smile. This practice teaches them not to greet a person with a sloppy touch of the hand, and grumpy face, looking the other way. In addition, it is a good way to make the contact between teacher and pupil, and makes both feel like friends for the rest of the day.

The children should feel free to choose their subject and their book or material, and to repeat some favorite manipulations as often as they like. On the whole, however, children of 8 or 9 and older prefer to follow a workbook, so they can monitor their progress and are aware which exercise they have to do. As each of them follows its own pace, and is probably working at a different subject from other children, there is not much opportunity even for short collective lessons, and difficulties have to be solved by individual coaching. Even if they can read, children at the first- and second-grade level need a great deal of help and reassuring. Their books need to be more frequently checked and their answers verified, whereas the older children can be given teachers' books to check the answers independently.

At the end of the morning the children should show their completed work to the teacher, who should write it in a book. This provides a constant view of every child's progress and enables the teacher to give account of it to the principal or a parent whenever necessary. At the end of each term or school year the teacher can also look at his notes and write a fair report on every child's progress. From these notes can also be seen when a child has been dwelling too long on one subject, neglecting some other (e.g. doing only math and no spelling exercises or vice versa). In most cases this happens when they come across some difficulty they do not want to admit or when the book they are using is too difficult.

To encourage the children, the teacher should ask them each day to make their own assessment of the effort they have put into their work: putting in a red mark if they thought they worked their hardest, blue if they worked not so hard, yellow when they thought their effort was poor. It is surprising to see how scrupulously fair is the children's judgment of themselves.

Some educational writers, including Montessori herself, maintain that children can make the teacher's task easier by teaching each other. This may be acceptable at the preschool age, but when it is a question of explaining why this or that is done, or even quoting a rule to go by, very few children can be relied on to give the right help. Some children simply fill in the answers in their schoolmates' books themselves, without a word of explanation, whereas others do not like to interrupt their own work to assist a classmate and refuse to give any help at all. On the other hand, children can be of great service by giving someone a dictation, testing his reading ability or checking the math exercises from an answer book.

Some teachers may disagree, but I never try to give a Montessorian "lesson of silence" — that marvelous physical and spiritual experience — to children over 6 years old. To begin with, there are at that stage always some children who have never been in a Montessori school, and may consider that exercise too childish, and spoil its effect by not cooperating fully.   But there are ways of obtaining silence indirectly, and giving children the experience of absolute quietness by asking them to listen to the beat of their own heart, or to the drop of a nail or other light object.

On the other hand, it would be wrong to use such exercises in order to quiet a group when it is too noisy. All silence exercises, to be really effective, have to be done when the children are in the right mood and are ready to concentrate on being quiet, by both not talking and being motionless as well.   In other words, being silent is a positive exercise, requiring positive effort, and not just an absence of noise, while the mind is occupied with other things.

As for the question of stopping excessive noise in the classroom, I am inclined to believe Ashton-Warner that noise is not an evil in itself and that objections to it are made more often by the teacher than by the children. Besides, there are more effective ways of fighting noise than by direct suppression, such as provision of more air space, ensuring there is less tension and more absorbing individual occupation.   The really obnoxious noise usually comes from individuals who walk about complaining: "I have nothing to do!" but who decline to do anything that is suggested by the teacher. When the normalization process begins to work on them, they gradually learn to be busy all the time, and to become quietly absorbed by their work.

A teacher who is really concerned about children — as a Montessori adept should be — cannot limit his activity to mere teaching of skills and knowledge that parents are unable to give their children. As previously mentioned, the learning process is closely connected with the development of the child's mind and character, with its ideas and emotions and its attitude toward the outside world[62]. This is why the teacher's role is so important, although often unappreciated, because his daily efforts and contributions to the children's mental and moral progress are not on public view. The teacher will often not get any thanks from either the parents or

The Montessori Lesson of Silence (Gatehouse School, London).

Each child quietly getting on with his or her own work (Gatehouse School, London).
Photos: Scott Thompson, London

his supervisors for his loving care and innumerable attentions aimed at keeping his pupils on the path to perfection. The children themselves will soon forget the benefits they received from him at this early age. But the teacher will have the satisfaction of having taken part in what matters most of all: shaping individuals and building a healthy society — slowly and patiently, brick by brick.

6

Other Educators

The teacher is not the only person responsible for the Montessori education of the children. There is the teacher's aide, and there are the higher authorities, namely the director of studies or principal or administrator, and the school governing body. And last but not least there are the parents.

THE TEACHER'S AIDE

The teacher's aide may be a certified Montessori teacher doing a 1-year internship, a state-qualified teacher without Montessori qualification, or simply someone interested in children and willing to be trained on the job. Whoever he or she happens to be, the aide must accept that two things concerning his or her functions will be taken for granted: First, the aide is in need of inservice training and must be prepared to learn — if only to coordinate their attitude and actions with those of the main teacher, because it is the teacher who carries the responsibility for the environment, the program and the way the children are taught. Second, the aide is as much an essential member of the teaching team as is the main teacher, and is indispensable for the successful progress of the Montessori class. Without the aide's dedicated assistance, the main teacher may become overstrained and exhausted, resulting in diminished efficiency. Therefore, the aide is expected to work to full capacity, taking an equal share of the teaching work.

One may think that having two teachers in a class that normally should not exceed 15 to 20 children amounts to overstaffing, and makes Montessori education too expensive. On the other hand it should be borne in mind that children in a Montessori class are meant to receive completely individual attention and tuition, to enable them either to move ahead, unrestrained by the average level of the class, or to slow down to a moderate tempo if they prefer, never to be rushed nor prevented from proceeding at a pace suited for them.   The children thus have the opportunity for unlimited progress both in quantity and direction, so that no child is neglected, but each is able to develop fully its positive potentials, having the environment tailor-made to suit its personality. It is almost as if every child had a private tutor, a luxury that normally only the most privileged families can afford.   This may appear costly, but the outlay is well worth it because of the results obtained by this method. In a properly run Montessori school, the children make very rapid progress in every direction.   A Montessori school is actually better than having a private tutor, because a tutor cannot compensate for the lack of social environment provided by other children.

Even in a well-trained class, the teacher and his aide are fully occupied, going from one child to another, helping one, encouraging another, and keeping an eye on general order at the same time. At times, one of them may have to give a child some lengthy explanation, and since the others cannot be kept waiting, there must be someone attending to them in the meantime. No workbooks are ideally written, and there are always some children who need to be shown how to understand the instructions and make good use of the materials provided. Having children line up at the teacher's desk, waiting for their turn to be helped, is not fair to the children and may lead to disorder.

At lunchtime also, two teachers are needed to take turns attending to the children, so that each of them can have at least a 1-hour break to relax and possibly prepare some materials, correct work done by the children, write notes, and so forth. To have a different person in charge during lunch or break-time is not a good solution. The teacher must be with the children both during the study periods and at the time of relaxation, observing them, helping them, playing with them and learning to understand them better.

Finally, there will inevitably be times when a teacher falls ill. At such times it is better that the class should be under the care of the other regular teacher rather than in the hands of a stranger who might upset the routine and cause disruption in class.

The aide must have full teacher's authority in dealing with children, and should be considered by them as equal with the teacher. This calls for a good understanding between the teacher and aide, because each must be ready to back up the rules and actions of the other — at least in front of the children — and in any case of transgression, each should personally enforce discipline without sending a child to be reprimanded by the other. In case of any conflict or difference of opinion in educational matters, no argument should ever take place within the children's hearing. The main teacher's opinion should normally prevail, especially if the aide lacks proper experience, but if it is not possible for them to agree, they should either bring the matter to their superior or get an expert Montessorian to arbitrate. However, it is better to come to an amicable compromise because of the inevitable repercussions of any dissension in the minds of the children. Also, if a teacher commits an error he is entitled to an opportunity of finding it out himself, in the same way as the children; and as long as the aide is devoted to his or her work, the positive influence of their personality may compensate for any lack of expertise.

The teacher and the aide should be jointly responsible for the maintenance and improvement of the environment. They should decide on some regular periods outside school hours when they can work together for such a purpose (say half an hour before or after school). They can also use this time for coordinating their methods and making plans for the days and weeks ahead. Once agreed on, these arrangements should become part of their regular duties, and the school authorities should be notified of them.

A regular feature in every school should be to have frequent staff meetings. In my opinion 1 or 2 hours should be set aside each week outside of school hours (without the presence of children) to discuss matters of common interest, coordinating methods, smoothing out children's transition from one class to another, and making plans for the future. If there is nothing to discuss, it should be a social meeting over a cup of tea or coffee,. This promotes unity and friendship among staff members and helps make them feel like a family.

THE TEACHER'S SUPERVISORS

In addition to the teachers, there are others who indirectly influence the children, by the authority they have over the teachers, their training, supervision, appointment or dismissal. They can be called by the general name of teacher supervisors. Some of them may not themselves have been teachers at Montessori schools, even if they are acquainted with the principles of the method. According to how they use their power and influence, they can help or impede and frustrate the teacher and the children, sometimes unwittingly. Whoever they are, and in whatever way they divide their functions, supervisors should keep in close contact with the teachers, know their methods and the times of their presence in school, and should as far as possible be acquainted with individual children and follow their progress.

One of the most important functions of a supervisor is to relieve the teacher of too much pressure from parents who may make exorbitant, sometimes conflicting, demands, or who may consume the teacher's time after lessons, when they are in need of a break. For example overprotective parents may wish to be reassured that their children are not exposed to harm, or ambitious parents may be reluctant to believe that their children are progressing satisfactorily if they are not ready for the math or science lessons of their grade. Supervisors can act as a screen for such problems and either give the parent the right answer at once, or undertake to discuss the matter over with the teacher first, or arrange for the parent meet with the teacher directly. The supervisor therefore needs to know the teacher well, and also his methods, and his effect on the children.

If there is a need for an error to be pointed out to a teacher who nevertheless acted in good faith, it is important not to make them feel hurt or offended. The supervisor should bear in mind that progress is often a slow and painful process, and that it is greatly dependent on the teacher having a quiet and serene attitude that gives children a feeling of security and confidence. If the teacher's peace of mind is perturbed by undue pressure, or if he or she feels strained, worried, or insecure in their job, it is bound to react on the children. Sensing a change in the teacher's attitude, they will resist instead of obeying, and regression instead of progression will be the result.

In fact, the atmosphere of the whole school should be like the one we expect to prevail in the Montessori classroom. The relationship between the teacher and his superiors should be one of confidence, trust, and mutual respect, like that between teacher and children. On the other hand, the supervisor should willingly listen to the teacher's complaints and sympathize with his problems, giving advice and encouragement. The supervisor should welcome the teacher's initiative in trying out new ideas, and allow him the joy of creating some new device or carrying out a new plan. He should respect the teacher's freedom to choose the materials and books. He should not even insist on the use of certain Montessori materials if the teacher does not like them. He should bear in mind that the teacher will make better use of those in which he has confidence, even if they are not designed for use in Montessori classes. Not unlike children, the teacher must always be creative, otherwise he will either become authoritarian, insensitive, and hard, or indolent, lazy, and inefficient.

At the same time, teachers should not be expected to spend their free time in making new materials, composing directions, and so forth. It is not their job to be an author, inventor, and manufacturer as well as teacher. If they are overworked, they will not be fit to teach properly the next day. However, if they do work after school hours out of personal enthusiasm, they should be made to feel that their work is appreciated, and any expenses incurred should be reimbursed.

If the teacher proves to be immature, inexperienced, or lacking in self-confidence, the supervisor should try to help him improve or put him in touch with someone who can. A good way of evaluating a teacher's quality is to watch the children's attitudes toward him. Children are the best judges of a teacher's competence!

However, the teacher's difficulties may arise from sources beyond his control. The question of whether a disruptive child should be retained in school despite the risk of causing regression in other children's behavior, is one instance when the teacher has no power to decide. Another problem can arise when the parents of a child insist that it should be forced to do more work. They should be told frankly when they bring their child to school that in a Montessori school children are encouraged to work, but never forced, otherwise their work will never become spontaneous. This is one principle that cannot be compromised, otherwise the school could not function in the Montessori methods, no matter what equipment is used in the classroom. The supervisor should explain this directly to the child's parents. A teacher should not be left with the dilemma of either having to act against his principles or losing his job to pacify a parent.

For obvious reasons, the school staff should not be composed of people of a single gender, age, or race. Although having the same teachers for many years can result in a loss of mental fertility, leading to stagnation, frequent staff changes are not good for the children either. They can cause emotional stress and difficulty in adaptation to each new person and different demands and way of teaching. The same goes for the practice of taking a child unceremoniously out of a school to which it has become accustomed, making it leave friends, playmates and the teacher, often without a chance of saying good-bye! When adults too easily change their affections without serious motives, the reason may well lie in some brusquely disrupted attachments in early childhood.

People who train Montessori teachers should be sure to insist on their having a deep understanding of the method's principles, more than an accurate knowledge about the use of its traditional materials. There may be alternatives to the well-known Montessori "Pink Tower", "Cylinder Blocks", and sensorial materials. Some of these may be equally good, or even better, than those recommended by Montessori. Everything is potentially improvable. The same applies to the more advanced teaching aids for primary or high school grades. As long as the teacher sticks to his way, and demonstrates it convincingly, there is no reason to impose a different method on him. In the end, it is practical experience that matters most, and Montessori would have been the first to agree.

PARENTS

No school can be successful unless there is deep and sincere cooperation with the parents. For the sake of their own children, if for nothing else, parents should keep in touch with the school, try to get acquainted with the Montessori method and the way it is applied in their children's classroom. The first initiative, however, must usually come from the school. Open days, informal discussion meetings, study groups, and other occasions should be provided to make the parents interested and involved in the school's life. Contacts of this sort, apart from creating general goodwill, can give the school authorities and the staff an opportunity for tactfully finding out all relevant details of the children's previous history, schools, or nursery schools they had previously attended, the reasons for turning to Montessori, any difficulties experienced in their education, the family circumstances (e.g. a deceased parent, separated or divorced parents, or both not living harmoniously together etc.) and anything else that can help staff understand and possibly anticipate problems that may arise in school. The teacher should be fully informed about all details that may help explain a child's character, its behavior, and its needs.

Apart from exceptional circumstances, parents should not be encouraged to help in teaching, or observe the children in the classroom, nor even to enter the class during school time. The reason is, in the first place, because unless they are teachers themselves, they probably lack the necessary experience and training to appreciate what is going on in the classroom, and why. Second, their emotional ties with their children may cause conflicts and prevent them from being accepted as teachers by their own offspring. And in case of their being a failure, it may be a delicate matter to tell a parent that he or she should stop coming. On the other hand, parents themselves often need advice regarding their children, how to deal with discipline at home, and with other problems. They may need to be told how to keep the children creatively occupied instead of letting them spend hours watching TV, how to avoid trouble at mealtimes, how to make going to bed easier, and so on.

Parents are often intolerant of their children's behavior, forgetting that adults are not saints either. Adults also have moods, do not always keep good resolutions, leave clothes and papers lying about, speak in unduly loud voices and have outbursts of bad temper. And yet, adults expect children, those frail creatures who have not yet had a chance to be educated, to behave like angels! Montessori said that children emerging from the age of the absorbent mind (about 6 years old, but in our sophisticated conditions in an urban environment probably earlier) pass through a difficult stage before settling down. It is particularly important at this time that home and school should keep in close contact. In order to occupy children after school hours or during weekends and holidays, the teacher may allow them to take some work home, say, whatever they like best doing at school (not what the teacher thinks they need to do most: which would look like a punishment), and the parents can be shown how to help them. In addition, there are many things which there is never enough time to teach at school (e.g. telling the time on the clock, reading the temperature from the thermometer, counting money in the purse and checking the change, learning the sounds of letters phonetically, and help with reading new words). These can well be taught at home. Parents can also be of great assistance in providing transportation for field trips.

As parents become more interested and actively involved in the educational process of their children, they may be more willing to contribute, each according to his means, to the enrichment of the environment, adding to the playground equipment; offering to give or lend some books, an atlas, a globe, a mirror for the bathroom (the need of which is often overlooked where small children are concerned), a plant or pet animal, a football or even a few old tires (an excellent toy with many uses in the playground!) and other items that are commonly discarded as useless, but which children can make use of.

It is not always easy to get the parents to attend meetings or to induce them to read educational books, however much they may need to be educated in this way. But a few enthusiastic parents may be persuaded to compile a monthly newsletter in which, apart from listing coming events and other school business, short articles can be included about childrearing.

In recent years, many schools have been started as parent cooperatives, with a view to cutting down the expenses a private Montessori school may require. This sounds all right in theory, provided that all the members of such a cooperative are well acquainted with, or willing to learn about, the Montessori method. Unfortunately, this is rarely the case. In practice many people send their children to a school without realizing that it commits them to accepting the methods used and playing their part in cooperating with them. If the methods used do not bring the results they expected, they may blame the school, harass the teacher or even use their power on the school board to have him removed. This type of situation can impose considerable strain on the teacher, who is faced with the task, first of all, of re-educating denormalized children to learn to discipline themselves, as well as bringing them to the point of voluntarily agreeing to do their school assignments. In a school managed by non-professionals who want almost immediate results in return for their money, there is a danger that the principles that it is supposed to uphold will be thrown overboard, so that it remains Montessori only in name.

The private elementary school is particularly exposed to pressure from outsiders because it is expected to achieve better results than the public schools. And yet, the children attending the private school are quite likely to be those which a public school has refused to accept: brain-damaged, hyperactive, emotionally disturbed, or having other learning disabilities requiring special treatment.

CONCLUSION

No school is entirely free of problems resulting from the failings of human nature. Apart from problem children, there are problem teachers, problem parents, and problem supervisors and directors. There are some difficulties of an internal nature that cannot be impartially judged and resolved by members of the staff or even by the school board. Regular and frequent visits by a Montessori-trained consultant (at least once a month, but preferably more often), should therefore be an established routine in every school, and the consultant's reports should be acted on.

A common cause of trouble in parent cooperatives and other small and over-ambitious schools is a lack of adequate funding. The yearly budget does not make provision for unexpected expenditure or sudden withdrawals of pupils, and when money runs out, cuts have to be made in books or equipment and staff salaries. The main sufferers are ultimately the children. It might perhaps be a good idea if no teaching license were issued to any school unless it is able to show that an adequate sum has first been deposited with trustees as a contingency in case of need.

It all boils down to the fact that to be successful, a Montessori school must have financial stability and a peaceful atmosphere. The school's ultimate purpose is not solely to provide children with knowledge, but to create a new type of human being, and a new and better society.

Only through a concerted, peaceful, and enthusiastic collaboration of all those concerned with education: supervisors, teachers, parents, and the children themselves, can that ideal be attained.

7

Further Reflections

A few further questions, connected with the problems of primary education, lend themselves to discussion here.

COMPARISON WITH THE "OPEN CLASSROOM" SYSTEM

The "open classroom" system of child-centered education is sometimes confused with Montessori. The term itself is somewhat imprecise. Roughly speaking, it means a break with traditional methods of whole-class "chalk and talk" teaching, and the adoption of a more elastic educational program, more adapted to the needs of children. Some open classrooms reject every rule set in advance and let children learn what they like, when they like, and only if they like, with the implication that some children may not learn anything at all. In some others, the "openness" consists merely of having no walls between classes, but otherwise pursuing the conventional type of same-for-all collective lessons.

In his book entitled <u>The Open Classroom</u>, Kohl conceded there is no single model open classroom; rather there are as many variations as there are combinations of students and teachers[63]. The book provided no clear definition of open classroom teaching, but gave the impression that he advocated a complete absence of any program imposed by the school. Advocates of open classroom education rightly point out that as long as an educational system is based on fear of punishment instead of voluntary self-discipline, it is likely to break down as soon as the child ceases to feel the watchful eye of the supervising teacher. Montessori would have agreed whole-heartedly. But this is only half the equation, and without a means of engendering that self-discipline, it is likely to lead to a propensity for adult delinquency and vandalism.

Nor did the book offer any guidance as to what a teacher is supposed to do if some children refuse to do any work at all, spend their time in chattering, tumbling on the floor, wrestling, shouting, and disrupting the concentration of those who are trying to learn despite such unfavorable conditions. Most teachers know the result if such a situation is allowed to continue unchecked: Children who are unable to concentrate and find no interest in learning soon become bored, make the wrong use of materials and books, damage the teaching equipment, and continue misbehaving deliberately to find out how far they can go with relative impunity. Such a situation is a recipe for chaos and low achievement.

The Montessori approach takes the view that children cannot be allowed to go adrift. They need directives, and a program to follow, and should be expected to make their own study plans and keep on learning of their own accord, systematically, undistracted by other options, and never flinching in the face of difficulties especially at some harder phases of work.

No serious learning can ever be just one beautiful path with pleasures all along the way, and society has the right to expect a quality and high standards of education, for those children will one day become its adult members. Unless they are properly prepared for that future role, willing to work hard, successfully competing for worthwhile jobs, obeying the rules of the company for which they work, and adapting themselves to the requirements of their trade or profession, they will become a burden, if not a danger to the community. Consequently we must, in the last few years of schooling, according to Montessori's own words, tighten the discipline in order to prepare adolescent children for the conditions of life in an adult society.

Montessori's idea of freedom does not leave any doubt about its true meaning. Liberty, she said, does not mean the freedom to do anything one likes, but the ability to act without help[64]. In other words, she gave the child the freedom to work in whatever way suits it best, so that it can develop creatively. This did not include the freedom to do wrong, however. The teacher must know exactly what plan to propose to the child once it freely agrees to follow his suggestions. It is up to the teacher to create a general atmosphere of enthusiasm for learning, creativity and cooperation, so that no child will ever want to stay idle. In such an environment no child will feel neglected, unrespected, or unloved, but will on the contrary be proud to participate in the common effort — even while recognizing that the ability and achievement of different individuals is bound to be unequal.

This way of teaching does not mean making all learning soft and easy. What it does mean is that the individual tasks are neither too hard and discouraging, nor too boringly simple. Each child is able to follow its own line at a reasonable pace, slowing down or speeding up, and choosing this or that subject. It is a process that gradually prepares the child to face the harder tasks of adult life, accept responsible positions, and overcome difficulties with courage, wisdom, and trust in the future.

Such is the Montessori way of education, open but not loose, free but with reservations, safeguarding order, forging ahead but always mindful of the way children react, develop and progress, in accordance with their nature.

WHEN SHOULD MONTESSORI EDUCATION END?

Another question that needs to be answered is whether the Montessori method of teaching should come to an end at any particular age.

The answer is that it should not, because the principle of positive education applies to any age. It is, after all, surely universally true that whenever we want to teach someone effectively, we need to prepare a suitable environment, and make our teaching attractive and reasonably easy to understand. We also need to encourage the students, whoever they may be, to acquire the knowledge they need as far as possible independently, using whatever sources of learning that may be available to them.

Montessori's own ideas concerning the education of older children were explained in chapter 3. A few further suggestions may be mentioned here.

Montessori took a particular interest in the problems of adolescents at that age when, owing to their awakening sexuality, they find it difficult to concentrate. Her medical training made her aware that at the age of puberty the intellectual strain should be eased, giving way to more emphasis on physical activities and the development of manual skills. She thought that, without stopping intellectual studies altogether, children at that period of life should spend a few years in the country, and be given opportunities to undertake some daring tasks requiring courage and ingenuity, and to taste adventure and a life close to nature. Later, between 15 and 18 years of age, they can return to serious study, and acquire the knowledge and skills needed for their future adult occupations.

The early teenage period of life was, in Montessori's opinion, so different from the preceding one that she gave children of that age a special name, taken from the German language: Erdkinder (literally, Earth-children or children of the Earth) in contrast to the previous phase in which they were Mobelkinder (literally house-furniture children). We could call them respectively children in the home (in the earlier period) and children of nature (in the later one).

Montessori never worked out a detailed program of education for the Erdkinder, nor did she name a precise age when one should start to put it into operation. In actuality some children begin that phase at a rather early age and give trouble at home and in school by being unable to concentrate on intellectual work. Yet similar ideas to Montessori's have been put forward by other pioneers and educational reformers. One of the closest to Montessori's thinking in this respect was Ernest Westlake, who advocated the concept of a school where children could live a primitive, adventurous life on the Red Indian model, while at the same time working at a normal school curriculum during school hours.

In the rural area of the old "New Forest" in Hampshire, England, a residential school of this type was founded between the wars, under the name of Forest School, and survived until World War II. Under the inspired leadership of its headmaster, Cuthbert Rutter, the children were encouraged to practice camping under canvas in the open, or sleeping in a barn on the bare floor, to trek for days over the countryside, light fires and cook their meals on them, ride on half-wild New Forest ponies and play adventurous woodcraft games, sometimes until late at night. The children were divided into age groups called Elves (under 6 years of age), Woodlings (under 12), Trackers (under 15) and Pathfinders (up to 18). Staff and older people in the community were called Wayfarers. Each children's group had an adult leader who was in charge of both teaching and outdoor activities. Girls particularly were fond of riding. Some of the 9-year-olds used to catch their ponies running free in the paddock, and bridle and saddle them without adult help. After passing some tests of their equestrian skill, they were allowed to ride the ponies around the school estate by themselves.

All children and staff took part in domestic chores such as cleaning the rooms, washing dishes, and lighting the open fire in the assembly room. Each group had its own room for its meetings, which they could paint and decorate as they liked. There they would discuss some of their problems, plan future excursions together, and spend their leisure time. A general school assembly, comprising both adults and children, dealt with matters concerning the whole community and drew up home regulations. Every member of the school, whether child or adult, could speak and vote during these meetings.

The school was a coeducational boarding establishment with no class distinctions between teachers, children, and domestic or schoolground workers. Everyone was called by his or her first name. Once every 2 or 3 months, all the children would be asked individually to write their views on themselves, their progress in study and other activities, and their opinion of the school and of other community members. Contrary to what might have been expected, this practice did not lead to recriminations, quarrels, or vindictiveness, but instead led to a frank and surprisingly positive and impartial evaluation of individuals, from which even the group leader and the head of the school were not excluded!

Although attendance at lessons was not compulsory, in practice the option of staying outside and playing during school time was hardly ever taken advantage of. Cases of insubordination and "playing up" teachers were rare and generally only occurred when a new child joined the community and carried on some behavior learned in a previous school. The culprits soon stopped being uncooperative when they saw that their schoolmates did not seem amused and did not support their disturbing antics. Any cases of serious or persistent antisocial behavior were brought before the assembly, where the transgressors were asked to justify themselves or accept some punishment devised as a logical consequence of their action

A school assembly meeting at Forest School, England ca. 1938 (the author at right rear).

The author coaching a child in math, using the Lubienski Arithmetic Board.

(e.g. someone persistently leaving the door open on entering a heated room in winter had to stay right at the back, far from the fire; someone refusing to take their turn at washing the dishes had to eat their meal alone, and so on). In general, however, having to stand accused before the whole assembly was a sufficient deterrent, and the mere threat of bringing someone to this kind of court was enough to bring the culprit to order.

Regrettably, in 1940 the danger of invasion by the Germans during the Battle of Britain forced the school to close, and after the end of the war it proved impossible to revive it. Many of the pupils, however, remained in contact with the staff and often came back to spend camping vacations in the old school grounds, nostalgically reliving memories of past days that many of them regarded as the happiest of their lives.

There was one feature that pervaded the whole life of the Forest School community, one that guided all major decisions. I call it a spiritual outlook. It was a religious sort of spirit that stressed the positive, good side of human nature, believed in its existence in the depths of each person and appealed to it whenever someone's behavior deviated from moral principles and gave physical or mental pain to other people.

Services held Sunday evening had no definite pattern, and followed no particular faith or denomination. But their influence was visible, and it permeated the whole life of the school. Whenever a problem arose at a staff meeting or general school assembly, it was significant how after discussion a solution reflecting a constructive and loving attitude was unanimously accepted by all.

Forest School never regarded itself as a Montessori school, and it had no Montessori material, but this positive attitude and the respect for the fundamental goodness of a child's nature made the school Montessorian in spirit. Which brings us back to the importance of a positive attitude in education, mentioned in the first pages of this book.

THE UNDERLYING PHILOSOPHY OF THE MONTESSORI METHOD

Talking more concretely, we can ask what was the basic idea underlying the whole of Montessori's scheme of education, the philosophy ruling her entire system? Looking through her numerous writings, I find one general principle logically arising from all her ideas. It is the affirmation of a need for the development of creativity and spiritual freedom in the child, and consequently in every teacher and everyone else in society. Freedom, after all, is the essence of life, necessary for the development of the mind as much as air is for that of the body. Hence, true, deep education cannot take place without it. Our whole life, in a way, is but an educational process that people must continue throughout their lives if they want to survive as rational beings. But to learn truly and deeply, one has to be free, like Montessori children.

Nothing could be worse for the Montessori movement than if the method should become crystallized into a rigid pattern, so that one could say with precision that one way of teaching is Montessori, whereas another one is not. There are some adherents of Montessori teaching who think they are doing good service to the method by trying to protect it from all attempts to modify or improve it, however slightly. Montessori used to complain about the harm done to her system by well-intentioned people, quoting an Italian proverb: "I can cope with my enemies, but God save me from my friends!" It is useful to recall this maxim when faced with a somewhat too rigid application of Montessori techniques that were, after all, introduced at the beginning of this century, not counting their previous use by Montessori's predecessors. What really counts in Montessori education is the ability of the teacher to help the development of a normalized personality in children through the process of free learning.

The normalizing process involves both the intellect and the subsequent free action, hence it changes and improves the whole personality and character of the learner. But it can be produced by a variety of means. There is, therefore, no reason to stick slavishly to traditional materials and methods unless they are proved to be superior to the new ones.

Four studies of the Dottoressa, from young to old. Photos: Top left, Biblioteque Nationale, Paris. Others, Association Montessori International, Amsterdam, Holland.

Montessori's greatness lay in the fact that she saw in her system more than a set of materials interesting to the children, because she knew that these could and should be improved on and replaced by others. She saw in it even more than an elaborate way of presentation of these materials to children, which explained mathematics by concrete manipulations and used ingenious ways for teaching reading, writing, and grammar.

No, her greatness lay in her aim of transforming all the world's children, and through them the whole of humanity, by making them love their work. In the Amsterdam series of lectures, mentioned in chapter 1 of this book, she unfolded her vision of a spiritual regeneration of the adult world through the growing ranks of the new children. In the last lecture she developed that idea still further. She said that, for human beings, work is a necessity, indispensable for remaining healthy. Work carried out in harmony with the laws of nature is not tiring. Flowers are not tired by blooming, nor are the stars by revolving in the sky's firmament. Work is the purpose of life, more important than life itself. Whenever individuals shrink from work, they bring disaster on themselves. The greatest error in education is preventing children from working spontaneously. Educators should protect children's individuality by giving it what it needs most: independence and work (in the right kind of environment, of course).

Just as the child is engaged in building the adult, so does the adult work at building society. How wonderful would a society be if it were composed not of slaves of organized labor but of tireless workers loving work above anything else!

What the world really needs, according to Montessori, is spiritual freedom. It is in this sense that we should understand her call, in the finishing words of her international course for training Montessori teachers in London in 1933:

We have given freedom to the child. Now we must give it to the adult[65].

8

Epilogue

In the later years of her life, Montessori developed some philosophical corollaries from her educational system. She felt that in a future civilization, spiritual values would take precedence over purely physical ones, and that humanity had an opportunity of becoming regenerated through a new way of educating its children. The following are her words from an article reproduced in the <u>Montessori Notes</u> of April 1935:

> While under the illusion of being highly civilized and morally strong, humanity today is in reality oppressed by its own environment. What it believes to be the strength of civilization is but an empty shadow of illusion, cast by the emptiness within.

> Up to the present, only one small side of man's whole personality has received the encouragement to develop strongly: that from which physical comfort can be derived. Mechanical intelligence has reached a high point of development in the creation of objects and devices to save labor, at which man gazes with satisfaction and pride as they accomplish his work, being active in his place.

> But while this small aspect of mankind's complex human nature has been cultivated and developed, the fundamental forces of life have been led into inertia: and with the passing of time that which is called "spirit" has remained stationary in development, while around it have grown up the powerful and mighty walls of what we call civilization.

> The inner side of man, and its laws of development, have remained as at the bottom of a deep well where a stunted growth has produced a retarded and false development.

Thus mechanical creation has been separated from the spiritual growth that should have inspired it; and thus enormous obstacles have been strewn upon the path to a superior life.

Childhood is simply the first period of a mankind that has sacrificed its own development for that of its environment; what is clear to one who, guided by long experience, can read its history, is that there has been a gradual and continuous sacrifice of man's inner energies for the triumph of external things. A complete revolution is necessary: the human conception of values must be reversed, and that spirit which is the creator of individuality must be developed, to soar aloft and dominate over and above all other human values.

Montessori was confident that this revolution was coming, that it was in the process of being realized in our time. In another article, extracts from which are presented in my translation from the Italian, she wrote the following inspired and prophetic words:

That the child's nature shows different characteristics from what it was believed to be, has been confirmed by experience everywhere ... not only in nearly every nation of our civilization, but also in every race, among them American Redskins, African natives, inhabitants of Siam, Java and Lapland. ... What impresses one is the difference of that human nature, the fact that it holds out the promise of producing better human beings. Is it then possible to change human nature? I believe it is indeed possible, and achievable in the following way: by substituting a "normal" condition for the deviations usually induced in children during their developing stage: and by giving back to man his mental health. If individuals are brought up in a healthy psychic atmosphere, so as to arrive at a full development, with a strong character and a clear intelligence, they will no longer harbor moral principles that are opposed to each other, nor simultaneously support two divergent systems of justice: one that protects life and the other that destroys it. Nor will they cultivate in their hearts the two opposing qualities of loving and hating; nor give their heart to two disciplines: one that unites human energies for construction, the other that unites them in order to destroy. A new world, for a new man: that is the paramount necessity.

If this statement were a Utopia, a joke, it would be sacrilegious to utter it, poised as we are on the brink of an abyss, at the bottom of which lies the catastrophe of the human race. But no, for at the beginning of this century a spark of miracles appeared on our globe. Is it not true that man can fly? Henceforward no land impediments will be able to separate one country from another any more, and man can circle the earth without invading another's territory. And if mankind can overcome the earth's gravity and reach into the stratosphere, who is going to be its owner? Who will have the rights over the gravity of the earth or over the ethereal covering beyond the stratosphere? The energy of the sun will be changed into a greater abundance of bread, and into warmth for human dwellings: now, which nation will declare itself the owner of solar energy? There is no limit to the new riches that man can acquire, searching the ethereal lights, the infinity of the sky, the starlit soul of creation. Well then, what possible purpose can there be for human beings to fight among themselves?

Until now, man has had to sweat while tilling the soil like one condemned, like a slave, restricting his greatness. But now that he has invaded the starlit sky, he can arise in all his greatness, to show himself to the universe as a new creation.

The CHILD! The new child is in him: man, who has overcome the third dimension, is predestined to go onwards for the conquest of the infinite. This is the vision of the real condition of our aerial times: we, the last two-dimensional people, must make a great effort to rise up and understand it. We find ourselves in a crisis, between an old world which is ending and a new world which has started already and has manifested all its constructive elements. The crisis we are undergoing is not a mere transition from one era into another. It can only be compared with those biological or geological epochs in which new beings appeared, of a higher and more perfect order, while on earth conditions arose that had never existed before . . .

Man meets no obstacles now in reaching any part of the globe, right to the most remote corners of the earth: neither mountains nor seas can stop him, because he can fly above them.

Who will sound the trumpet that will wake him? What will man do, he who now lies asleep on the surface of the globe, while the earth is about to engulf him?[66]

The answer is clear: it is the children, the new children, who will wake him, the ones freed from the shackles that until now have prevented them from working spontaneously, according to their true nature.

Appendix

Suggestions for Equipment*

SUGGESTIONS FOR OUTSIDE EQUIPMENT

1. What is important above all in the playground is to have ample space for children to run about, chase each other, race, play any spontaneously conceived games, or jump up and down. If there are any grassy patches and little mounds in the grounds, so much the better. Children between ages 6 and 12 require more than four times the space that preschool children are satisfied with. The playground should be at least 60 feet square per class. For rainy days, there should be a large hall with gymnastic equipment where the children can play and make as much noise as they want.

2. It is not enough to have climbing frames for these children. They adore climbing trees, or some sort of framework requiring a little daring, even if it is quite safe otherwise. There should be some high swings, a slide, a horizontal roundabout, thick boards fixed in the ground sideways for walking on like on the line in a junior Montessori classroom and, if possible, some water that can be directed down a slope with dykes, bridges, and tunnels made according to the children's fancy; possibly even a place where they can safely make a camp fire, collect firewood, and learn how to light it, and so on.

3. Some space should be set aside with soil for growing flowers, vegetables, or other plants, either individually or collectively by a group of children. Another, larger plot should be left for adventurous digging, making a landscape, constructing a windmill or a shed with old boards — all the things that children love doing as soon as they are

---

* Equipment is listed in order of importance

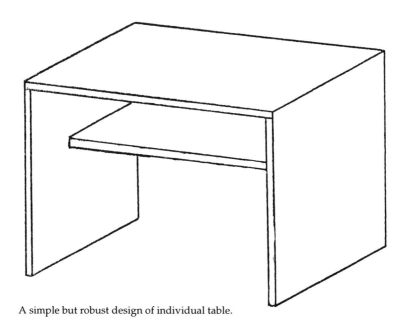

A simple but robust design of individual table.

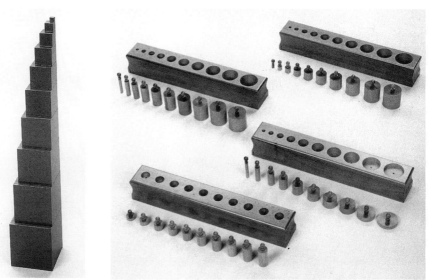

The Montessori Pink Tower (left), and the Montessori Cylinders (right). Photo: Nienhuis Montessori, Zelhem, Holland.

strong enough to lift a shovel. Add to it a few dozen old bricks, and they will soon make use of them to build a little house of their own.

4. An old shed or disused building, if available, can be useful for keeping tools: spades, hoes, saws, choppers (for use only under staff supervision of course) and possibly some materials for painting and decorating walls, wallpapering or plastering them and drawing some graffiti. These places could be used for some secret meetings, and so on.

5. A sandbox, of reasonable size of course.

6. Some accessories for outdoor play, such as old car tires, barrels, wooden crates, drums, and one or two rubber balls.

7. A kiln for firing clay work. If proper safety precautions are taken, a fairly efficient one can be made out of an old dustbin, by making holes all round about 2 inches apart and filling it with hardwood sawdust. The clay models can be placed in the center and the sawdust lit. It will burn itself out within 1 or 2 days, depending on weather conditions, emitting slight, inoffensive smoke, and the models will come out hard, ready for painting and glazing.

INDOOR EQUIPMENT: MAJOR ITEMS

1. Individual tables and little chairs or benches. Each child should have its own table, and there should be some space between the tables, so that none of them touch each other, unless it is necessary for some purpose. Going by experience, the tops of the tables should measure about 24 x 18 inches (60 x 45 cm) to allow room for some teaching materials as well as exercise books or paper to write on. There should be a shelf about 5 inches (12 cm) below the tabletop for keeping pencils and books not currently in use. The sides of the tables, reaching from the top to the floor level, can be made of wide boards, about 20 to 24 inches (50 to 60 cm) high, according to the children's size, so there need be no proper "legs." This type of table is both practical and strong, and easy to make.

2. A cabinet with cubbyholes, each about 12 inches (30 cm) wide, 6 inches (15 cm) high, and 10 inches (25 cm) deep, so that every child

has one for storing its worksheets and currently used books. This arrangement enables the teacher to distribute the daily assignments easily and supervise the children's work.

3. A long table or set of wide shelves on which to display children's work (e.g. clay models, drawings and other items).

4. An electric clock placed in a prominent position, so that each child can see the time.

5. A sink and faucets for hot and cold water (apart from one in each lavatory) with wide draining boards and suitable cleaning materials for water experiments and washing dishes, clothes, and other items.

6. A perforated board, fixed over the sink or in another suitable place, on which various tools and other objects can be hung.

7. A large bulletin board for the teacher's or children's notices (not to be used for children's drawings, favorite pictures, etc., for which some space on the walls or an indoor partition should be reserved).

8. Several easels for painting on large sheets of paper.

9. A board (or wall space) for hanging artwork to dry.

10. A blackboard (which need not be of black color) for chalking by the teacher or children.

11. Several small looms for weaving, with a supply of wool in various colors. Additional looms can be improvised by using the backs of suitably constructed chairs.

12. A cupboard or suitable space for materials for sweeping, dusting, polishing furniture, decorating and so on.

13. A copier for duplicating flyers and the like.

14. A first-aid kit with instructions for those who want to practice using it. The kit should contain adhesive bandages, scissors, peroxide, cotton balls, and so on.

15. A variety of building blocks in attractive colors (e.g. Legos) that can be used on a rubber mat, so that if any fall on the floor accidentally not too much noise is made.

16. A typewriter with supplies of typing paper, carbon paper, and envelopes.

17. A record- or tape player with a selection of records or cassettes.

18. Two room thermometers, one indoors and the other outside a window where it is not exposed to the sun.

19. A barometer with an adjustable hand showing the last reading.

20. A large globe of the world.

Apart from the single items listed above, there should be collections of learning materials in special parts of the classroom or in special rooms with glazed doors separating them from the main room:

1. A reading corner, containing selected books either owned by the school or borrowed from a library. The books should include a junior encyclopedia, an English dictionary, and other reference books. It should have comfortable chairs and cushions to sit on, and be a specially attractive and cozy place.

2. A natural history corner with installations for growing indoor plants and experimenting with seeds. There should be a fish tank, and possibly a cage for some small animals or birds that the children can feed and keep clean easily. Reference books concerning animals and plants should be kept handy.

3. A Math corner with concrete math apparatus such as Montessori, Cuisenaire, Unifix and so on, and both manual and electronic calculators; scales with decimal weights, and a collection of small objects to weigh and to "sell", price lists for shopping, imitation money, and the like; also other equipment for mathematical calculation, measuring, preparing geometrical drawings, and so on.

4. A Science corner with a number of basic materials and graded instructions that children can easily understand. Also some relevant reference books and magazines.

5. A Social Studies corner containing a good atlas, maps of the town and surrounding area, jigsaw maps (with names of the territory written at the back of each piece), appropriate workbooks, reference books, and all the stationery needed for enlarging maps, drawing graphs, making models of geographical features, and so forth, a good compass, some tracing paper, and so on.

6. A kitchen corner with a few saucepans, a frying pan, and a gas or electric cooker, some cups, plates, cutlery and essential foods easy to cook, simple recipes and instructions for handling the cooker and food.

7. An arts and crafts corner where children can find materials for drawing, painting, modeling, and other crafts taught in the class as well as for improvised creations. In addition to paints, brushes, sewing and knitting materials, etc., there should be a "treasure chest" filled with all sorts of discarded objects, such as boxes of various sizes, wire, string, bits of leather or cloth, spools, tubes, and various items usually thrown away by tailors, printers, or plastic workshops. The inventive mind of children can use all such articles for making such things as airplanes, ships, motor cars, dress ornaments, and any other items suggested by their imagination.

8. A heavy tool corner (not to be used during study periods) with a carpenter's bench and manually operated tools for wood and metal work, a lathe, a potter's wheel, and a supply of corresponding materials.

9. A corner for educational games, including any items that develop the mind and require thinking, whether for several people or one person alone, but not for winning by pure luck: checkers, dominoes, various mathematical or language games, chess, scrabble, jigsaw puzzles (graded from easy to complicated, but not requiring more than one afternoon session to complete), various matching and memory games, and so on.

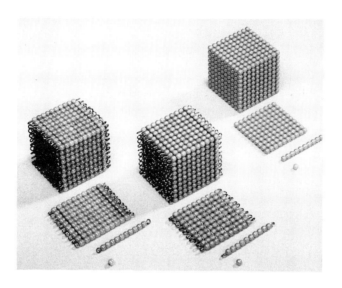

The Montessori Golden Beads for Arithmetic.

The Montessori Buttoning and Tying Frames. Photos: Nienhuis Montessori, Zelhem, Holland.

10.A music corner with a piano and a repertoire of suitable song and books. This should preferably be in a soundproof room or in a hall where dancing lessons can take place.

In addition to these areas, there should be a cupboard or set of shelves for keeping materials temporarily not in use or kept for repair or the replacement of lost pieces. This is best located outside the classroom and kept under lock and key.

There may be reasons for having lavatories close by, with doors opening directly from the classroom.

If funds are available, it may be useful to have the following additional items:

1. A darkroom with equipment for developing photographic films and printing them.

2. A film projector and screen.

3. A small printing press with letters manipulated by hand.

4. A sort of grandfather clock, with weights and adjustable pendulum.

5. A large "landscape tray" filled with sand or clay that can be wetted and shaped into various geographic configurations with mountains and valleys, islands, canals, volcanoes, industrial, or agricultural districts, and so forth. Additional materials may be kept to feature grasslands, forests, rural or urban areas, and so on.

INDOOR EQUIPMENT: MINOR ITEMS

In addition to the equipment just listed, there are a number of items without special location, that nevertheless have to be kept in stock to be used wherever they are needed. These include some Montessori materials to which even primary stage children like to return, such as the color tablets, sound cylinders and other sensorial materials, the movable alphabet letters, reading, writing and grammar materials, the Golden Bead material, multiplication and division boards for work with beads, the chains of beads for skip-counting, the Seguin boards (called Arithmetic Frames in Montessori's handbook), and the elementary geometrical figures (square, triangle, and circle) divided into sections.

Common Items

In all departments, however, some articles of stationery are indispensable, and it can be very frustrating when an activity is delayed because of lack of some common items that have not been thought of. There should be always a supply of the following:

1. Loose sheets of writing paper: plain, lined, cross-ruled, and graph paper.

2. Water paints at least in the three primary colors (red, blue, and yellow).

3. Paint brushes (long and medium size).

4. Staplers of several sizes with a supply of staples.

5. Good quality scissors — plenty of them.

6. Some all-purpose glue in small containers because children have a tendency to use far more than is necessary.

7. Large sheets of strong paper (to be cut to smaller size when necessary) for painting on with water paints or felt-tipped markers.

8. A good paper-cutter (not to be used by children without supervision).

9. Sheets of cardboard of various thicknesses in different colors.

10. A good supply of carbon and tracing paper.

11. Erasers.

12. A good supply of pencils (medium soft).

13.Pencil sharpeners.

14.Ball-point pens with caps — blue, red and black (a good supply).

15.Sets of assorted colored pencils (not crayons, they break easily and do not make attractive pictures).

16.Folders of various colors.

17.Transparent scotch tape.

18.Masking tape (a good supply).

19.A few letter-weighing scales.

20.Sets of felt-tipped marker pens in various colors, if possible the kind that can be revived by dipping in water.

21.Paper clips (fairly large size).

22.Paper fasteners (the type that perforates the sheets of paper to be held together).

23.Assorted elastic bands (a good supply).

24.A few staple removers.

25.Thumbtacks — of the sort that can be easily removed without breaking one's nails (if not, a thumbtack removing tool to be added to the set of tools).

A set of handy tools: a light hammer, pliers, several sizes of screwdrivers, a box with simple nails, picture nails, screws, hooks, and so on.

Many more items could be added to this list, of course, and equally many of those listed here may have to be omitted because of lack of space or financial resources. Every school has to make its own selection of materials according to its needs, and gradually increase them as its needs grow and change. It takes many years to develop a satisfactory environment, but it never remains the same for long because new ideas and requirements bring constant changes and improvements (and that is how it should be).

Subject-Oriented Materials

A few words should be said about the choice of materials of the Montessori type for learning different subjects. It is true that a vast number of teaching aids are available in the shops, and the catalogues of educational suppliers are full of them. Yet comparatively few of these materials are the sort which can truly be called Montessori-oriented. It is therefore important for teachers to have some guidance as to what to look for when deciding on the purchase of materials for their class.

Let us start with materials for teaching mathematics, particularly those intended for developing the first ideas of dimension, quantity, serial order, number, and other concepts that are the basis of all computation. In order to discover the secret of success of early Montessori mathematics materials, I tried to analyze the best of their kind and described the results in an address to the English Montessori Society in January 1969[67], quoting five typical traits that characterized them. Later, I reduced these to four, namely that they should be simple, dynamic, as far as possible self-corrective, and of course attractive to children.

Simple

Materials should be simple, both in design and in the way they are to be used. This has many advantages. A simple material is easy to understand and to apply, it can be adapted to many uses, and it is usually easy to manufacture and sell at a reasonable price, even though it is essential that it be accurately made, especially in mathematics. A typical example of simplicity of this kind can be found in the Montessori Cylinder Blocks or in the Pink Tower, and among Montessori-oriented materials in the Geoboard.

The Cylinder Blocks consist of long blocks of wood into which a number of round holes have been drilled, each different from the others either in diameter or in depth or both. Cylinders of corresponding size have to be fitted exactly into the proper holes. The Pink Tower is a structure built with cubes of gradually diminishing sizes from a height of 10 cm in the bottom cube to only 1 cm at the top. The Geoboard is a square with nails driven into it at regular intervals, looking like a square crossword puzzle made of 100 little squares with a nail in each corner. Elastic bands are provided to stretch around the nails and form various geometric and nongeometric figures.

All three items just described can quite easily be made with simple tools in a small carpentry workshop. They provide fascinating exercises for toddlers, serving to develop both finger control and intelligence. On the other hand, they can also be used with older children for teaching the decimal system, for comparing areas and volumes, explaining the multiplication table and fractions, and so on.

Dynamic
The second feature, the dynamic quality of the material, is the most important. The material should not be chiefly designed to be looked at (such as ready-made figures in plane or solid geometry), but must be of the sort that can be manipulated in order to solve problems and discover new relationships. Children using this material in spontaneous exercises may sometimes discover things not even thought of by its designers. It is evident that the three types of materials already described are definitely dynamic, meant to be used as tools of learning rather than as illustrations of a ready set of theorems and principles to be learned by heart.

Self-Corrective
The self-correctiveness of a material is a feature much valued by Montessori, chiefly because it makes the child independent of the teacher, preserves the child's pride and doesn't oblige it to compare its achievement with that of others. If a child puts a cylinder in the wrong hole, there will in the end be another piece left over, which will not fit into the remaining space. Likewise, in constructing the Pink Tower, if the child puts a large cube on top of a smaller one, the tower will eventually collapse; in any case the child will feel that the total shape looks different from the one he dismantled in the first place. (In traditional Montessori schools the Pink Tower is always left standing erect in its place in the classroom.) On the Geoboard, too, the student can find his mistake, say by comparing the size of a rectangle with that of an equivalent triangle, or by counting the little squares within the areas contained by the elastic bands.

Attractive

Finally, the material has to be attractive, well finished, colorful and pleasant to handle, otherwise the children will not like to use it. Montessori always took great care to have her materials made to be exquisitely beautiful.

These characteristics of mathematical materials can serve as a guide for selecting suitable teaching aids for other subjects, such as language, spelling, social studies, and science. They will all give better results if they are simple, dynamic, and attractive, and even if they cannot have a built-in control of error, children can have access to the answers contained in the teachers' books.

The author, shortly before his death in 1997.

Index – Correction Table
Please subtract as follows:

Quoted Page No.	Subtract	Quoted Page No.	Subtract
1 – 15	0 or 1	76 – 90	5 or 6
16 – 30	1 or 2	91 – 105	6 or 7
31 – 45	2 or 3	106 – 120	7 or 8
46 – 60	3 or 4	121 – 135	8 or 9
61 – 75	4 or 5		

Index

Endnotes

[1] One of the best, although still incomplete, descriptions of the Montessori method is given by Orem. He wrote that the Montessori method is designed to help each child to develop fully as a whole person at its own natural rate of progress through freedom of expression in an environment prepared to fill its physical and psychic needs. Self-development, self-assurance, self-discipline and self-realization are the keynotes of the Montessori approach.

R.C. Orem, Montessori. G. P. Putnam's Sons, New York 1974, pp. 97-98.

[2] Dr. Montessori's message. Montessori Notes, London, July 1935.

[3] Hélène Lubienska de Lenval made some interesting comments regarding the problem of technique versus philosophy of education in her book La Méthode Montessori (Editions Spes, Paris 1962) in a chapter entitled "Métaphysique Montessorienne".

[4] See Orem, op. cit. p.103: She [Montessori] held that the true nature of an ideal early education (and in fact all education) was largely self-education. . . . Other educators had proclaimed its validity before her. But she was the first to develop such an extensive program of specific techniques for its implementation.

[5] Hélène Lubienska de Lenval actually discovered the original material created by Seguin and later adopted by Montessori in the hospital of Bicètre, France, "in a dusty old cupboard." It was in that hospital that he applied them to mentally retarded children. Montessori modernized the objects and replaced leather with fabrics, and metal pieces with wood, but the concepts were fundamentally the same. See Hélène Lubienska de Lenval, op. cit. p. 24.

[6] Maria Montessori, The Montessori Method. Schocken Books Inc., New York, 1964, p.373.

132

[7] The Secret of Childhood. F.A. Stokes Company Inc., New York, 1939, pp. 126 and 136-7.

[8] Translation from a French article by Maria Montessori in the Journal de Genève, March 7, 1932.

[9] From an article by Montessori in the Manchester Evening News (England) May 3, 1932.

[10] Sylvia Ashton-Warner, Teacher. Simon and Schuster 1963. The whole fascinating chapter entitled "Creative Teaching," pp. 27-100, is worth reading and reflecting on.

[11] The Montessori Method, p.28.

[12] From personal notes taken by Hélène Lubienska de Lenval at a lecture by Montessori in Geneva in 1932.

[13] From the French article by Montessori in the Journal de Genève (see note 8).

[14] The Secret of Childhood, p. 215.

[15] Montessori Notes, June 1935.

[16] Journal de Genève, as in note 8.

[17] Translations from an article in the Italian magazine "L'idea Montessori", June 1927.

[18] Maria Montessori, Psico Geometria. Casa Editorial Araluce, Barcelona 1934, pp. 9-10. Translated into English in Montessori Notes of May 1935. See also the same idea, expressed sometimes in identical words, in the Rivista Montessori of May/June 1931, pp. 5-6.

[19] Montessori Notes, October 1935.

[20] Some concrete examples of the stages in children's way of thinking have been analyzed in Jean Piaget's studies on the development of children's intelligence. However, he warned that the advent of each new stage does not abolish the thinking processes of the preceding stages, so that new ways of reasoning are simply superimposed on the old ones. See "The Origins of Intelligence in Children." Newton and Co., New York 1952.

[21] See Montessori's article entitled "The Four Planes of Education", in the Bulletin of the Montessori Society in London, Spring 1967.

[22] Ibid.

[23] Ibid.

[24] Ibid.

[25] Ibid.

[26] Ibid.

[27] Ibid.

[28] Ibid.

[29] Ibid.

[30] Ibid.

[31] Ibid.

[32] Ibid.

[33] R.C. Orem, Montessori, p. 167.

[34] Ibid. p.121.

[35] Rivista Montessori (Rome), March/April 1932, p. 80.

[36] Translation of a passage in an article by Montessori in French, entitled "La Nouvelle Maitresse" [The New Teacher] in The Call of Education.

Psycho-pedagogical Journal, International Organ of the Montessori Movement, edited by Maria Montessori. Amsterdam, vol.II no.1, 1925.

[37] See the Montessori words quoted above in note 6 and the interesting article by Barbara Edmonson entitled: "Let's do more than look — let's research Montessori" in "Communications" published by the Association Montessori Internationale (AMI) in Amsterdam, Holland, December 1965.

[38] The Secret of Childhood, p. 107.

[39] Rivista Montessori, May-June 1932.

[40] The Advanced Method. Heinemann, London 1929, vol.I, p. 87.

[41] The Montessori Method, pp. 349-350.

[42] Ibid. p. 369.

[43] Ibid. p. 376.

[44] Op. cit. p.93.

[45] Ibid. pp. 96-97.

[46] Ibid. pp. 99-100.

[47] Children, the Challenge. Duell, Sloan and Pearce, New York 1964. p. 277 ff.

[48] The Open Classroom. A New York Review Book. Vintage Books, New York, 1969. p. 51, Note.

[49] Teacher, p. 104.

[50] Ibid. p. 63.

[51] Ibid. p. 56.

[52] Ibid. pp. 103/104.

[53] Ibid. p. 15.

[54] Ibid. p. 105.

[55] Whether the teacher himself (or herself) is religious or not, they must surely agree that to be grateful to others and to God can help anyone feel better, less angry, more secure and more friendly — in short, that to induce such a sense is both good education and good psychology.

[56] Reprinted in Montessori Notes, Winter 1970.

[57] Montessori Notes, July/August 1934.

[58] Teacher, p. 11.

[59] The Four Lives, p. 66.

[60] The Open Classroom, p. 13.

[61] Ibid. p.29.

[62] See R. Dreikurs, Psychology in the Classroom. Harper and Row, New York 1968, p. 277. The author said:

> Teachers and schools ... cannot discharge their duty to impart academic knowledge unless they understand the whole child and help it in its adjustment. ... We must go ahead and devise means by which we can stimulate cooperation, responsibility, and growth ... making the school an enjoyable and rewarding experience for teachers and pupils alike.

[63] The Open Classroom, p. 55.

[64] The Bulletin, Spring 1967, p. 5. These words by Montessori are quoted from a lecture she gave in Edinburgh in 1938.

[65] From a private notebook

---

[66] Rivista Montessori, May/June 1932.

[67] Published later in the Montessori Journal (London) No.48, winter 1970. See also my earlier article in "Mathematics Teaching", organ of the Association of Teachers of Mathematics (England), No.25, winter 1963.